HORSE FEVER HORSE FEVER HORSE FEVER
HORSE FEVER HORSE FEVER
HORSE FEVER HORSE FEVER
HORSE FEVER HORSE FEVER
HORSE FEVER HORSE FEVER
HORSE FEVER HORSE FEVER
HORSE FEVER HORSE FEVER
HORSE FEVER HORSE FEVER
HORSE FEVER HORSE FEVER
HORSE FEVER HORSE FEVER
HORSE FEVER HORSE FEVER
HORSE FEVER HORSE FEVER
HORSE FEVER HORSE FEVER
HORSE FEVER HORSE FEVER
HORSE FEVER HORSE FEVER
HORSE FEVER HORSE FEVER

HORSE FEVER

HORSE FEVER

a guide for horse lovers and riders

BY PAT JOHNSON

A RUTLEDGE BOOK

GROSSET & DUNLAP · PUBLISHERS · NEW YORK

to girls and boys everywhere
who love horses
and especially to my nieces
Carol and Mindy

ISBN: 0-448-04489-0
1975 Printing
Copyright© by Rutledge Books
1961, 1962. All Rights Reserved.
Library of Congress
Catalog Card Number 61-6340
Prepared and Produced by
Rutledge Books, Inc.
for Grosset & Dunlap Co., Inc.
Printed in the
United States of America

CONTENTS

1 HORSE FEVER *page 13*

2 POPULAR SHOW HORSES *page 25*

3 THE WESTERN HORSE *page 37*

4 EQUIPPING YOU AND YOUR HORSE *page 43*

5 CARE AND FEEDING *page 55*

6 FIRST AID *page 63*

7 COMMON SENSE OF RIDING *page 71*

8 THE CROWNING GLORY *page 83*

Photographic credits:

Blue Meadow Stables, Westport, 74, 75, 77; Clove Lake Stables, S.I., 38, 47, 90; The Complete Book of Horses, 43, 81, 85, 86; Freudy Photographers, National Horse Show Assoc., 47, 86, 87; Ira Haas, Morgan Horse Club, 33, 49; Elizabeth Hibbs, 41, 43, 48, 52, 55, 60–61; Tad Horton, 24, 34–35; Irish Tourist Bureau, 51; Dept of Public Relations, Kentucky, 27–28; Carl Klein, 62–68, 75, 77; Frederic Lewis, 82, 83, 85, 87; Grete Mannheim, 36, 52, 54, 58–59; Monkmeyer Press Service (Engelhard), 29; (Henle), 27, 40; (Merrim), 37, 86, 89; (Palmer), 38; (Pinney), 56, 57, 75; Morgan Horse Club, 32; National Horse Show Ass'n, 31, 85, 88, 90; Palomino Horse Breeders Ass'n, 39; Tennessee Walking Horse Ass'n, 31, 50; Von Dwingelo, 13–23, 25, 44–45, 47, 70–74, 77, 78–79; Western Horsemen Magazine, 35.

Clothing on 44–45 by courtesy of M. J. Knoud Saddlery. Personal photographs on 20–21, 28, 42, 77 by courtesy of Miss Joan Draper; on 12 and 20 by courtesy of Dr. Manuel Gilman; and on 42 by courtesy of Mrs. M. J. Werber.

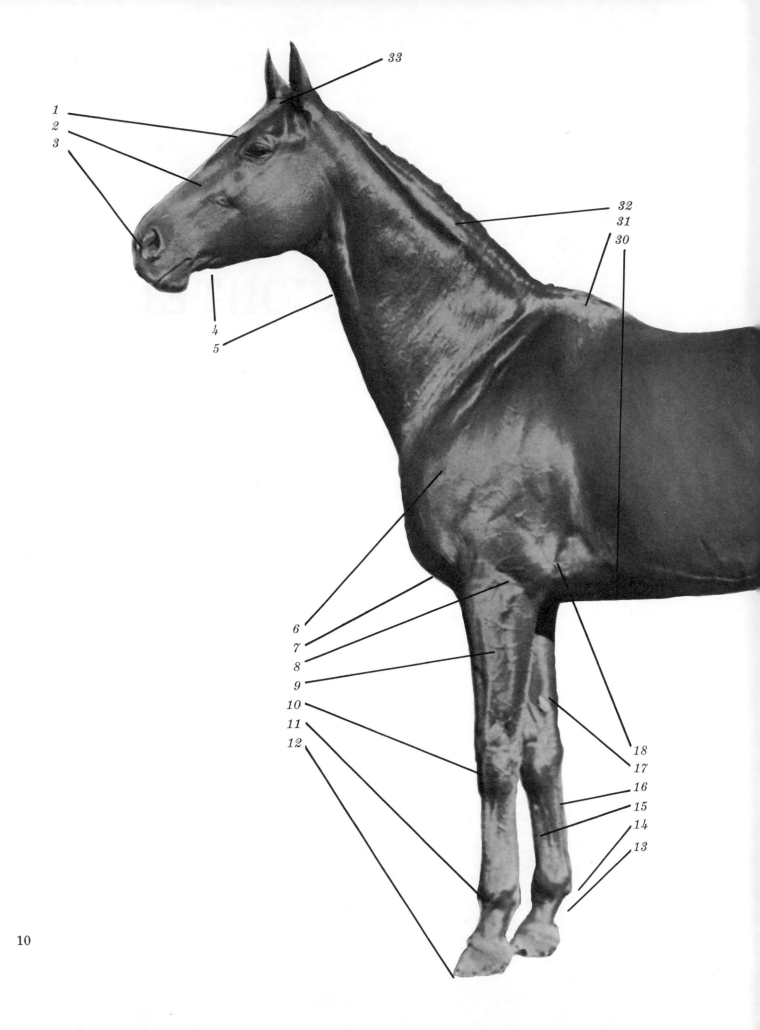

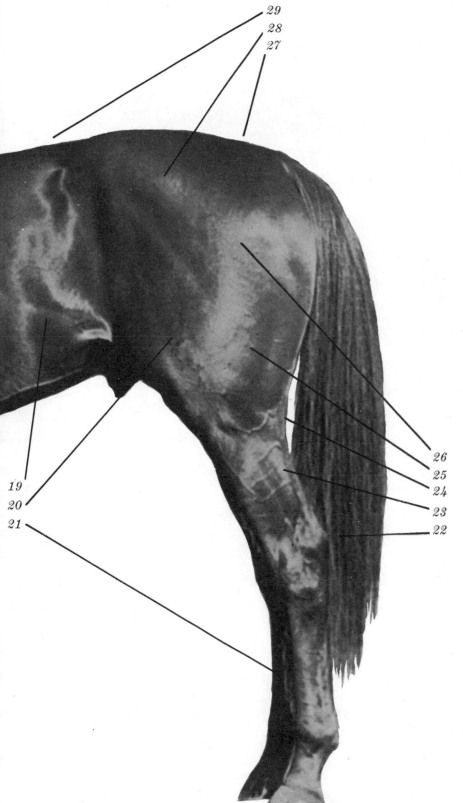

THE HORSE

1 Forehead
2 Face
3 Muzzle
4 Jaw
5 Windpipe
6 Point of Shoulder
7 Breast, Chest
8 Arm
9 Forearm
10 Knee
11 Fetlock Joint, Ankle
12 Hoof
13 Pastern
14 Fetlock
15 Cannon Bone
16 Tendon
17 Chestnut
18 Elbow
19 Flank
20 Stifle
21 Cannon
22 Hock
23 Second Thigh, Gaskin
24 Quarter
25 Thigh
26 Pelvic Terminal Bone
27 Croup
28 Hip Joint
29 Loins
30 Barrel, Body
31 Withers
32 Crest
33 Poll

HORSE FEVER

Have you ever been to a horse show and seen the sleek, shiny horses of every size and color performing at the peak of their splendor? If not, you don't know what you're missing. Come along now on a trip to the country, and the wonderful world of the show.

As soon as you start to bump along the old dirt road that leads to the show grounds, you'll feel excitement in the air. It's a kind of excitement like a light fever, *horse* fever. Anyone who likes animals loves horses, and almost everywhere you look you'll see horses—some being ridden in an easy, relaxed manner by seasoned professional riders; some being held by proud, smiling grandmothers; some acting frisky in the crisp morning air as soft-voiced grooms do their best to quiet down the snorting animals; some standing peacefully, gently nuzzling their affectionate owners.

Young riders will be scurrying in every direction, hunting for the proper number to wear on their backs so the judges can identify them easily, searching for their hunt caps or derbies before the next class begins, or maybe just plain trying to find mother. Other riders may be out for some early morning practice, putting the high-stepping Saddle Horses through a walk, trot, and canter. Or you may see a well-dressed rider in black boots and canary-yellow riding breeches taking a big, rangy hunter over the outside hunt course where the jumps are like the actual jumps a rider would meet on a real hunt. You'll hold your breath the first time you see that Thoroughbred collect himself and go up and over a four-foot stone wall with the ease and grace of a dancer.

Pounding away in the distance will be the rhythmic beat of the blacksmith's hammer, the ringing clang of iron on iron as he shapes a shoe. When the shoe is properly formed, the clanging will stop only to be replaced by the softer thud of a small hammer driving the nails through the shoe and into the horse's hoof. But don't worry about the horse being hurt. His hooves are like your fingernails. No pain is felt around the edges where the shoe is tacked on, any more than you feel pain when your nails are filed. Only if a nail is hammered too near the center of the hoof will a horse feel any discomfort.

As you keep moving along the dirt road, you'll see horse vans and trailers which transport the animals and equipment to and from their home stables. In the background, you'll see the barns where each owner is assigned stalls for his horses and, if the show is a large one, there will even be huge tents put up to stable the hundreds of horses that will be on hand to compete in the sport of kings.

But these days is it the sport of kings only? Not on your life! In fact, if you'll buy yourself a program and step right up to the rail of the big riding ring where the various events (each of which is called a 'class') take place, you'll discover for yourself that riding horses is truly becom-

At typewriter with notes near by, a sports writer taps out horse show news, headlines

A judge examines a hunter's conformation, checking his overall physical appearance

Judges, protected from sun and rain by a colorful tent, calmly discuss a competing hunter's performance

In an open jumping class, the horse that knocks down or touches the least number of fences wins. Here an entry clears a gate

Railbirds frown and gasp as horse falters

ing the sport of kids.

Let's take a look at the program together and you'll see what I mean. Suppose the first class of the day is the Lead Line Class. This class is open to young riders who are still beginners and whose horses are held on a 'shank,' or lead rope, throughout the class by an adult riding another horse. All the young beginning rider is asked to do is to walk and trot. The youngsters who enter the Lead Line Class are often only five or six years old. Such a class as this gives any new rider a fine start, a chance to gain confidence and poise.

You'll be wanting to know what's the next step after the Lead Line Class. Well, there is a whole string of Horsemanship Classes open to girls and boys under eighteen—designed specifically for young riders and suited to each stage of their development. Exactly what is a Horsemanship Class? It's an event in which the ability of the rider is judged. There are many other classes in which the performance of the horse is what counts. —and in such classes the rider may even resort to worsening his own rid-

ing style if he can show the horse to better advantage by doing so. Horsemanship classes are also called equitation classes, from the Latin word for horse which, as some of you know, is *equus*. It's from these events that the world's best riders get their basic training, and learn to ride in championship style.

Let's take a look and see if, at the very show you're visiting, we may not find one of the outstanding riders in today's horse-show world—eighteen-year-old Joan Draper, whose home is in Fairfield, Connecticut.

There she is, over there by the paddock fence, watching her younger sister, Margaret, perform in the Lead Line Class. Even as a little girl, Joan loved horses. She can remember how she used to pester her parents—constantly begging them to give her riding lessons. Her father is a veterinarian and understood her desire to be with horses.

When Joan was eight, her parents arranged for her to take lessons twice a week at the Fairfield Hunt Club under the instruction of Emerson Burr. Right away, Mr. Burr saw that Joan had a naturally fine sense of balance and felt very much at ease on a horse. As often as school work would allow, she practiced mounting and dismounting, and riding at a walk and a trot, and soon she was on her way to her first show. You know what her first class in a big show was: the Lead Line Class at the Fairfield Hunt Club Show—at the age of ten. Joan

A rangy gray takes a
perfect jump—thanks to free
head his rider gives him

Checking a jump for exact height

Here's your horse's name, right here!

19

The Draper family all set for a hunt   *Proud beginner on mount led by mother waits for start of lead-line class*

won second place—her first ribbon, a beautiful, big red one. Joan's as proud of that ribbon today as when she first won it, and since that show she has gone to win in almost every major show in the East.

In riding with an English saddle (as contrasted with a Western saddle), there are two main kinds of position —or 'seat'—you take when sitting astride the horse: the 'hunter (or forward) seat' and the 'saddle seat.'

Because Joan lives in the Connecticut countryside among gently rolling hills and New England's old stone walls, this young rider chose to ride hunter seat. You'll see the difference between the two seats in photographs on following pages. In learning to ride with this basic position, she prepared herself for jumping, because the hunter-seat position is used when a

rider goes over fences. Saddle-seat riders must be content with riding on the flat—no jumping.

"Saddle seat," says Joan, "is majestic and beautiful. But it's not for me. I like to be able to have fun on a horse, and I feel that a rider can do so much more with a hunter. A hunter is just as beautiful in the ring as any other horse, though he's certainly less flashy. He gives me a much better ride out on the trails where the going may get rugged. And then, there's nothing like knowing that you can jump right over a wall or fallen tree if you come across one out on the bridle path.

"And remember, if you ride hunter seat you're prepared for the unbelievable thrill of riding on a real hunt — chasing over the fields in the early morning with the pack of hounds

20

Joan Draper shows form that
wins championships: her head up, hands
forward, heels well down, legs
firm with toe and knee in line. At
left, she receives trophy presented by
Governor Ribicoff of Connecticut

21

streaming out before you."

There's no denying that Joan might get a few arguments from Saddle-Horse fans—especially those who feel that five-gaited horses, with their flowing manes and tails and showy extra gaits, are the crowning point in any show.

But what is a gait? Of course you know it's the walking step or the trotting step a horse uses as he moves along, but perhaps you aren't aware of the number of kinds of step a horse can take. A three-gaited horse is so called because he can walk, trot and canter. These are all called natural gaits. The five-gaited horse adds two movements, the 'slow gait' (a single-foot step in which each strikes the ground singly) and the 'rack,' a kind of fast single-foot. These gaits do not come so naturally to the horse as the other three—horses have to be taught to perform them. But we'll discuss these gaits in greater detail a little farther on.

But in spite of the showy qualities of the five-gaited horses, a great number and variety of classes are usually open to hunters, and Joan certainly knew what was right for her because, since that first red ribbon, she has

With graceful ease, a fine hunter and determined rider take a brush fence

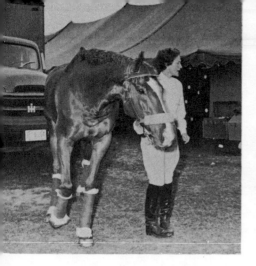
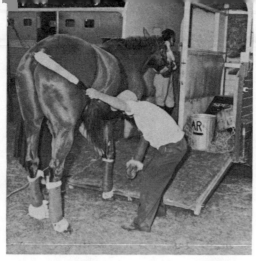

Though this horse needs coaxing, it's time at show's end to load up and head for home

won important awards. She was presented with the Champion Rider of the Year Trophy in 1956 by Governor Ribicoff, of Connecticut. She also won the 1957 High Score Award, presented at the American Horse Show Association Convention in New Orleans.

And just to prove that there is such a thing as horse fever, the entire Draper family now rides! They've gone from owning the one horse they bought when Joan was ten to owning five. Two of these are kept at the Draper home and Joan, who admits she's no early riser, points out that it's easy to care for them. For the simplest form of care, all you need is a shed or barn to serve as a rude shelter, an acre or two of fenced-in land as paddock or pasture—and a first-one-up-in-the-morning arrangement to take care of the feeding!

Of course, really superb care is more involved than that—and you'll find out more about it later. Then you can decide for yourself how fancy you want to be in your treatment of a horse. But don't let anyone fool you— just because horses are large, that doesn't mean they're hard to take care of. A horse is as simple to keep as a dog—and the rewards are altogether different. So get a good spot

at the rail during the show and keep a keen eye on those horses. Decide on the kind of horse that's right for you, depending partly on whether you know how to ride right now and how well, and on whether you want to buy a horse to keep permanently or one you will want to trade in after a while.

What appeals to you, as you watch each animal perform with his own special magnificence? Do you like the easy naturalness of the hunter? Or do you prefer the regal splendor of the Saddle Horse and the five-gaited horse? Perhaps you like the smooth rocking-chair comfort of the Tennessee Walking Horse, or the solid, taut strength of a Morgan. If you're looking for lovely color, how about a Palomino? If you want a sleek, true aristocrat of horses, be sure you pay attention to the Arabian.

If you're uncertain about just which sort of horse is right for you— let's go backstage at a horseshow. Let's see where people buy horses, how they take care of them, what equipment they need, how much things cost, and how they start learning to ride. Who knows if, given a little practice and a chance to show your determination, you may not become a champion like Joan Draper yourself!

23

POPULAR SHOW HORSES

2

Let's go horse hunting!

You've had a brief glimpse of a horse show and you know what fun it would be if you could ride in one yourself. Besides, you love horses and there isn't anything you wouldn't do to have one of your own: you'd promise to finish all your homework, keep your room in order, help with the dishes and other chores, be quiet and polite—and attend to all the things your parents remind you of during those moments when you know you aren't at your best. And you're determined to keep those promises for such a reward. So let's look around to see if we can find the right mount for you.

"But hold on there a minute," you may be thinking right now. "Horses are wildly expensive, for one thing,

and besides—what if my riding ability isn't so hot?"

Your fears on both counts are groundless! It seems as if horses must be expensive because probably the only ones you've heard about are the famous ones—race horses or champion show horses whose prices commonly run into many thousands of dollars. But there is a vast selection within the range of average-income families. These are the horses which give fun and friendship to thousands of children—and to grownups as well—all over the country.

For only fifty dollars you can get your own horse. He'll be a skinny, unkempt-looking animal, but you can feed and curry him back to health and turn him into a perfectly suitable

25

family mount. And there's always the chance that he may turn into a champion. Every now and again a weary-looking animal is rescued from misfortune by some keen-eyed horseman—and soon that very horse is discovered to be a fabulous jumper who secures triumphs and trophies for his owner.

For one hundred to one hundred-and-fifty dollars you can get a quiet, sound animal which would probably be outclassed at bigger shows but which would do well enough for you in small country shows—in 'hack' (trail horse) and horsemanship classes.

If your family can afford it, about three hundred dollars is a good amount to count on spending. At that price, you can shop around a little and find yourself a horse with plenty of promise—one that will do well in shows but will not be too high-strung or frisky for a youngster to handle.

However, if you don't think you can afford any outlay for buying a horse but you can afford to keep him (that is, feed and stable him), and if you have paddock space for him, there's another possible solution. Don't buy a horse at all; instead, get in touch with a large summer camp or riding academy and offer to take care of one of their horses after the camp season is over. Many camps realize how much young people love horses—and they would much rather have their animals given the attentive care of a loving child than send them off to public stables during the winter. For ten months of the year you'll have your own horse—and you won't have to pay a cent beyond his keep to get him.

Naturally it's helpful if you know your way around on a horse a bit because then you can see for yourself whether or not you like the gaits of the horse you are considering. You are in a position to rely on your own feelings for the horse's possibilities rather than on the opinion of a friend. Still, it isn't absolutely necessary for you to know how to ride before you buy. In fact, a quiet horse of your own —one that becomes used to you and fond of you—will help you improve your ability faster than practice on the sluggish, indifferent creatures you often come across at stables.

Now let's get down to the business of finding the right horse for you. Where do we look? Preferably at a breeding farm, a place which makes a business of the buying, breeding, raising, training, and selling of horses. First of all, a breeding farm will have a wider range of animals for you to choose from than any other source. Second, a successful horse breeder depends on his reputation. It is true that horse traders are apt to drive a hard bargain, but a breeder of fine horses will not deliberately set out to cheat you. Selling horses is this man's sole livelihood, and if word gets around that he's a shady dealer, he'll soon have no buyers. At a farm you can look over the horse of your choice at leisure, see how he behaves around the barn and with other horses, watch

Off to trails winding through rolling hills

Thoroughbreds and foals enjoy brisk run

him being bridled and saddled, perhaps go back two or three times to get acquainted with him, and generally not feel rushed into buying him.

Private riding academies are also good places to hunt for a horse—especially if you know the owner of a stable and have confidence in his ability to find a suitable horse for you.

Auctions are a third place for the buyer to hunt—but this is risky for the average person. Sales move fast, the horses are shown quickly, and you simply don't have a good chance to see what you are getting. Experienced horse traders can get good bargains at auctions, but such sales are usually too tricky for the unskilled buyer.

Once you have located a breeding farm near you and a couple of riding

academies where you can get a look at what each has to offer, it's time to ask yourself a few questions—questions which only *you* can answer. For example, do you want a horse just for you or one that the whole family can ride? Do you want an older, fully trained horse? Or do you ride well enough to be able to train a relatively unschooled horse? Whatever you decide, make it clear to the person showing you his animals that you want a quiet, mannerly mount. Then take your time to look over the field—and, as an added safeguard, take an experienced friend with you. Getting expert guidance in selecting your horse is vital. Find someone who not only rides well but who is a good horseman—a person familiar with the han-

27

Joan Draper goes over a brush fence on perfectly formed hunter Silver Science

Young horses tussle fondly while trying to shed halters they aren't yet used to

dling of horses, who can judge accurately the kind of horse best suited to you. Then, once you and your adviser have selected a horse, ask the breeder's or the stable owner's permission to have an animal doctor, or veterinarian, look the animal over. When you have the vet's okay, go ahead and buy your own horse.

Let us suppose you are looking for a hunter. Because hunters, both in chasing the fox on a real hunt and in taking the fences in a show, require speed and stamina and jumping ability, ideally you would try to buy a Thoroughbred. The Thoroughbred is a specific breed of horse, not to be confused with the term 'purebred,' which may be applied to any breed of horse and simply means that a horse is of pure bloodline. Through selective breeding, Thoroughbreds of today are horses of incomparable speed and courage—desirable qualities in a hunter. No horse can outrun a good Thoroughbred, but a hunter needs jumping power as well as speed. For that reason, hunters used in especially rough country often have more than a drop of draft-horse blood in them. Admittedly, for $300 you may not find a sound Thoroughbred, but you will be able to find a horse with Thoroughbred blood in him, and one that has many of the same characteristics.

His head should be wide between the eyes and should narrow down to a fine muzzle with large nostrils. (See chart p. 10.) His nose should be relatively straight, neither arching prom-

This solid hunter shows many traits to look for, especially the well-built head and neck

inently outward (a 'Roman' nose) nor curving greatly inward (a 'dished' face). The point where the head and neck join should be lean, and the horse's windpipe clearly defined. His neck should be long and slightly arched, and his shoulder long and sloping; this shoulder formation is important for it means a smooth, lengthy stride. There should be good depth along the girth line—between the withers, that prominent bump at the base of the horse's neck, and chest. The horse's back should be rather short and his hind quarters slanting rather than boxy. Just behind the shoulders his ribs ought to be more or less flat, but they should become more rounded as they continue back towards his rump. (Now turn to your chart.) His cannon bones should be short and strong, his pasterns fairly long and flexible, and his knees and hocks should be thick and sturdy. These are all parts of the horse's legs and their locations are illustrated clearly in the chart on page 10. His muscles should appear smooth and flat and, generally speaking, his bones should be long and light.

29

You must realize that these are ideal qualities. Don't expect to find all of them in the horse you can afford to buy. When you find a horse who has many of these good points, he should be 'tried out' so that you will know if his gaits are easygoing and comfortable, and if he is able to maintain a smooth, even speed when jumping.

The exact opposite of the fast, rangy Thoroughbred is the American Saddle Horse. Just as the Thoroughbred is a specific breed of horse and not a purebred animal of any given strain, so the Saddle Horse is a specific breed and not simply any horse broken to saddle and bridle.

There are two chief types of Saddle Horse—the three-gaited and the five-gaited. The three-gaited saddler is shown with his mane clipped off entirely and his tail shortened and shaved at the top. He performs the three natural gaits—the walk, trot and canter. (A canter is actually a collected gallop. Some horsemen maintain that the three natural gaits are the walk, trot and gallop, and that the canter is an artificial, or taught, gait. But nowadays most people agree that the canter is a natural gait.)

The five-gaited horse is usually shown with a long flowing mane and tail (p. 31) and, in addition to being able to walk, trot and canter, he performs two extra 'artificial' gaits—the slow gait and the rack. How are these two different from the natural gaits? Well, in a trot the horse automatically moves his diagonal legs at the same time. The left rear leg and the right foreleg rise and then hit the ground simultaneously. Pacers move both legs on the *same* side together. The right rear and the right fore leg rise and land at the same time. But the pace is a highly uncomfortable gait and is used only when a pacer draws a sulky, or small racing cart. In the rack the horse's rear legs pace while his forelegs trot. Confused? It's hard to picture the separate actions of a horse's legs. The important thing to know is that the rack should be a very comfortable gait which the rider sits to, just as he sits to a walk or a canter. The slow gait is merely a slow rack.

Both types of Saddle Horse are compact and generally smaller than the Thoroughbred—but they are not chunky animals. Their conformation (appearance) is elegant and showy. The saddler has a small, proudly held head, an exceptionally long and highly arched neck, and his arched tail is set high. His back is very straight and noticeably shorter than that of a Thoroughbred, and his legs are set well under his body. His shoulder is well slanted and his pasterns are very long and flexible, allowing the horse to have good action in his legs. Along the barrel, he is round, and his hind quarters are full and round—not sloping like the quarters of the hunters.

The Saddle Horse is bred for the show ring, so when you're looking around for one to buy, you should bear in mind these two points. First, he should be highly trained in picking up

A five-gaited horse with flowing
mane and tail performs at a rack. The
head is held high, the neck arched,
the legs lift gracefully with the long
flexible pasterns guarded by boots

A perfect example of one of the
South's loveliest products—the easy,
smooth-gaited Tennessee Walker

31

Note slightly 'dish' face that marks this colt as an Arabian

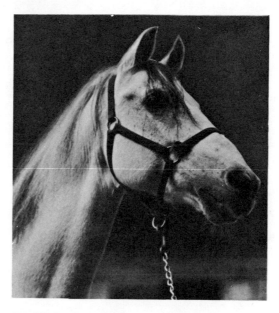

Springtime, and this herd of Westerns moves toward a favorite watering spot

Width between the eyes and pointed ears prove the Arabian blood in this horse

and his qualities have found their way to every part of the world. His speed and stamina were passed on to the Thoroughbreds but countless other strains are the heirs to his heroic endurance, his beauty and his phenomenal intelligence. He is a truly distinguished animal and is so treasured by Arab riders that he is often taken into the tent of his owner and treated as a friend.

Many points of the Arabian's conformation set him off from other horses, and when you look at him, you'll see that the shape of his head is one of the most obvious. His face curves in and is what we call 'dished.' His ears are curved and point toward each other at the tips so that they nearly touch. His eyes are large and protruding, giving him a wide area of vision, and they are set lower on his face than other horses' eyes. The Arabian's muzzle is fine, delicate and his jaw is deep. His back is also a distinctive feature, for it is unusually short.

When you consider the compactness of the rest of his body, the Arab's hindquarters seem rather long—and this contributes to his great speed. Swiftness also comes from the bone structure of his legs: his cannon bones are short and thick—a highly desirable quality in a speed horse.

The Arab's nature is gentle and intelligent. He can subsist on little food and is known to have great resistance to diseases—especially ailments affecting his breathing. In shows he usually performs at a walk, trot and canter and, as he circles the ring, you'll immediately notice his proud, aristocratic bearing.

Now, these are the chief show horses ridden in most shows and suitable for most young riders. Choose carefully and remember to get the advice of a veterinarian before concluding the deal. Then waste no more time. Buy the horse, prepare for the best time of your life, and enjoy it with all your heart.

35

3

THE WESTERN HORSE

Whenever the term 'Western horse' is used, most people picture a rough-and-tumble rodeo—an event full of color but so full of danger, too, that no youngster would be permitted to enter the regular events. What few people realize is that many small, country horse shows have classes open to Western horses. The wide range of these local shows gives them their importance to the show world, and if you own a Western horse, you should pay attention so you'll know about the shows in time to enter your horse.

In case you strongly prefer western riding, you don't have to worry about being left out of the fun—or change your style simply because you thought all horse shows were exclusively for English riders.

"Well," you may be thinking, "all I have to do, then, is to pick out the kind of horse I want and then use a western saddle and bridle on him. That's just fine."

But it isn't quite as simple as that! From what you've read so far about the different kinds of horse, you know that you wouldn't advise a person about to go on a hunt to use an American Saddle Horse on the chase. You'd suggest he use a Thoroughbred—or a horse with Thoroughbred characteristics. The same standards of suitability hold true if you're picking out a Western horse for yourself. Suppose that, during your excursions to find a horse, a big, long-limbed Thoroughbred strikes you as a handsome animal—one you'd like to own. After all,

Young Quarter Horse shows rounded muscles

Rider speeds by keg in a barrel race

you reason, he has speed, courage, stamina—just right for a Western horse.

True, the endurance and speed of the Thoroughbred are unquestioned, but still he is not what you'd want for western riding. Why? Because a good Western horse must have many other qualities. First of all, he must be a relatively small horse. Size is important because the working cow pony has to forage for himself when it comes to food. He must be able to do a hard day's work on the scant rations he can find to nibble on the plains. Irregular, limited feed would mean the end of any Thoroughbred—he would simply starve on the rough diet of the Western horse. Another count against the Thoroughbred is his length of limb. Take a look at his legs: they are long and slender—built for the lengthy, thunderous stride it takes to cover the hunt fields or races. Can you imagine such a horse trying to dart in and out of a herd of cattle, making sudden stops and quick starts, whirling turns and dashing sprints? Of

course not. The Thoroughbred would be all legs in such a situation. He'd no sooner catch his stride than you'd be jamming on the brakes, ready to dart out after some stray.

Can you think of a third strike against a pure Thoroughbred? What about his gaits? That long, springy trot would reduce any western seat to a pulp after a day's work on the range. Some day you try sitting to the trot of a hunter. It takes a good deal of skill and effort not to bounce. However, a cowboy must devote all his skill and effort to doing his job— he has no spare time simply to keep himself from bouncing. Thus his horse must have a comfortable walk and a pleasing canter, or 'lope,' as it is called in the West. (The Western pony is rarely called upon to maintain an extended trot.)

Well, having eliminated the Thoroughbred from the field, you might now begin to wonder what breed is right for western riding. Strictly in terms of breeds, the Morgan and the Arabian offer good Western-horse

38

These independent fellows are never as sleek as eastern horses

prospects. Both are small horses and have plenty of strength and endurance. The Morgan is compact and therefore good at making fast turns, stops and starts. The Arabian is traditionally a desert horse and so is capable of working on little food and foraging for himself. Also, he has a perfect canter.

However good Morgans and Arabians may be, an important western breed we haven't yet talked about is the Quarter Horse. Every Westerner will boast of the qualities of this breed, but the fact is that the Quarter Horse had his beginnings in the East—in Virginia. In the late 1600's, Virginia gentlemen enjoyed racing their stock but there were no big race tracks available. They would use stretches of road near the towns—the road lap usually being about a quarter of a mile long. The distance became standardized and men began to breed horses especially for these quarter-mile races. Usually the breeder combined imported English horses either with the speedy little runners devel-

oped by the Chickasaw Indians or with a Rhode Island variety which had come down from New England and competed successfully against earlier Virginia horses. Then a horse named Janus, an English racer with Thoroughbred bloodlines, was imported and began to transmit his characteristics to all his offspring. In time, the entire breed was influenced by the speed and power he passed on to his foals, and, as sprinters, Quarter Horses became unbeatable. Then, when race tracks were built, the Easterners gave up the Quarter Horse in favor of Thoroughbred racing on longer tracks. But ranchers and cowboys soon discovered that the compactness of the Quarter Horse enabled him to turn quickly and stop short. His large, rounded, muscular shoulders and hindquarters gave him plenty of drive and thrust so he could get off to a rapid start. That is why the Quarter Horse came to be almost every cowboy's favorite—and the breed has found a lasting home in the West. Nowadays, breeders frequently

A golden Palomino in western rig. Saddle and bridle are richly decorated for parade use

introduce more Thoroughbred blood into the strain so as to keep the heads of these large-quartered horses small and beautiful—like the head of a Thoroughbred.

Life is not all work and no play for the Western horse's rider. One of the most enjoyable moments in a cowboy's life is when he and his horse can take part in a colorful parade on a holiday celebration. And here is one area in which color and all-round flashiness are what capture the Westerner's heart. The Palomino is a type whose popularity rests entirely on the beauty of his color and, when it comes to choosing a parade horse, a rider will have to look long and hard to find an animal that can beat the Palomino in this field. If you buy a Palomino, you will find many opportunities to show him in parade-horse classes, where he may compete against horses of other colors as well as in classes open only to Palominos.

The size and especially the abilities of Palominos vary greatly—to such a degree that even eastern show-goers take an interest in this horse. True, where breeding has produced the features of the American Saddle Horse, the owner usually sticks to keeping the Palomino in parade-horse classes. But there are Palominos with hunter characteristics. These are generally schooled in jumping and entered in open jumping classes. In open classes, the horse's appearance and manner don't come under consideration at all. The winning horse is simply the one which clears the most jumps or has the least number of faults scored against him. As for the rider, any form goes in an open class—as long as the horse clears the jumps.

How do you pick a good Palomino? Well, since the main feature is his color, his coat should be nearly the same shade of gold "as a newly minted U.S. gold coin," according to the *American Horse Show Association Rule Book.* If the horse you choose is very dark—almost liver-colored—he may be successful as a parade horse but he will be penalized in straight Palomino classes. The same holds true if your horse is very light in color— almost as pale as cream. But light or dark, every Palomino should have a white mane and tail. In a show, the presence of dark hairs in the mane and tail will lower the score. As far as white markings are concerned, a Palomino may have white on his face and he may also have white socks— but if the white reaches above the hock in back or the knee in front, the horse will again be penalized. A horse with white marks on his body would be considered a Pinto—the Spanish word for painted, and indeed these horses do look as if white paint had been splashed on their basic coat color— and because of this would be eliminated from a Palomino class.

Now we have talked about the breeds most suited for western riding —the Morgan, the Arabian, the Quarter Horse, and the Palomino—but, if you want to buy a Western horse, the thing you should watch out for above all are his characteristics. A Western horse can be of almost any breed—or any mixture of breeds—as long as his conformation is suited for western riding. He should be a small, rugged animal so that he doesn't require much food. He should be compact so that he can be easily maneuvered, and his gaits should be comfortable. He should also be very muscular through the shoulders and hindquarters so he can stop and start quickly. If you can find a horse with these qualities, he'll make a fine Western mount. It doesn't matter whether or not he has the breeding of a Quarter Horse, Morgan, or Arabian. The only reason these breeds are important to know about is that they produce the desirable characteristics with great consistency. If you buy a Quarter Horse, you know you've got all the makings of a fine Western horse. Many people would rather have this assurance and rely on breeding than scout for a horse on their own and take a chance on an animal of unknown background. The choice is up to you.

As far as price is concerned, you'll get a better financial bargain, of course, if you don't buy a horse of any special breed. But in order for it to be a bargain, you must be satisfied that the horse you choose can do happily the things you want him to do.

4

EQUIPPING YOU AND YOUR HORSE

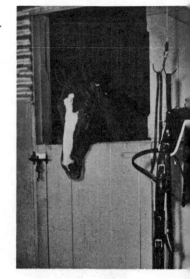

Now you have a horse of your very own—and he's due to arrive at his new home soon. Have you already named him? Have you pictured what that name will look like when it's printed in the program of your first horse show? You may even have thought of ordering a special sign that you can place right over his stall.

But whoa! We're getting ahead of ourselves. Name plates are a luxury, and before you even consider such refinements, you'd better think of all the necessities you'll want to ensure safety and comfort for your horse— and your riding.

First of all, let's talk about the things you need for yourself—but remember, you must not feel that you ought to go on a spree and buy all these items of equipment all at once.

Fortunately, equipment for yourself is limited. The only things you really require are the proper riding clothes for the horse show. If you ride hunter seat, the correct dress for a show (see photograph, p. 44) consists of: 1) canary-yellow riding breeches, 2) black boots, 3) either a turtle-neck sweater or a man's shirt and tie; other alternatives are a ratcatcher shirt and tie, or a ratcatcher shirt and stock, 4) a riding jacket, 5) a hunt cap.

These are what you'll need, so try not to get talked into buying anything else. What do I mean by getting talked into buying the wrong thing? Well, many misinformed parents and kids go to a store which sells riding equipment and decide to outfit themselves.

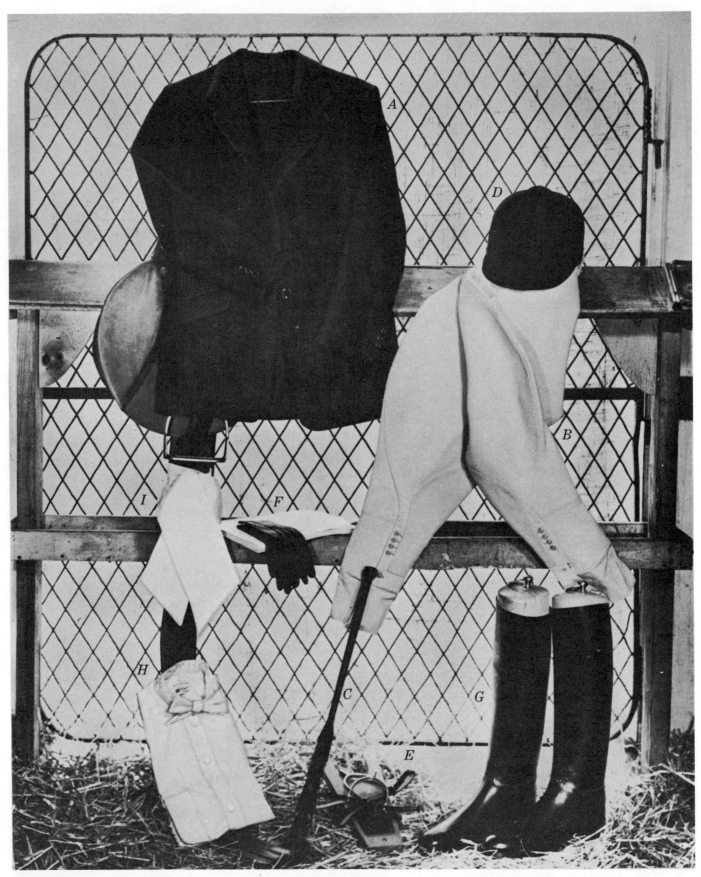

Complete outfit for hunter seat rider includes A-black jacket, B-canary hunt breeches, C-feathered bat, D-hunt cap, E-spurs, F-gloves, G-boots, H-ratcatcher shirt, I-white stock. When boots aren't in use, put tightly rolled newspapers in the legs to preserve their appearance and save the expense of boot trees.

Informal saddle seat outfit consists of A-jacket, B-jodhpurs, C-derby hat, D-jodhpur boots, E-gloves, F-riding crop, G-man's type of shirt. As veteran show-goers will tell you, no matter how clear the morning skies—be sure to take a durable raincoat with you whenever you go to a show to outwit showers.

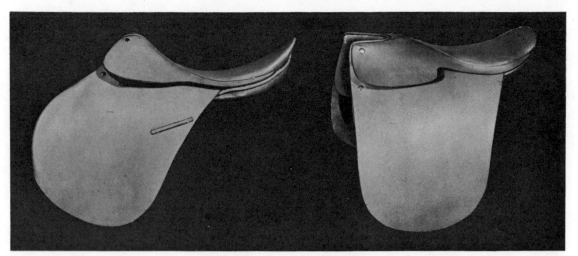

Hunter seat saddle has deep seat and knee rolls for jumping. Saddle seat saddle is flat

All too often they are confused by the difference between breeches and jodhpurs. Hunt breeches are wide at the thighs, having what are called 'pegs' which extend out from the right and left sides of the rider. Then the pants become narrow and fit very snugly from the knee down. Breeches do *not* continue down to the ankle but end several inches above and fasten with buttons, zippers or tie strings. Like breeches, some jodhpurs have pegs, but unlike breeches they extend all the way down to the ankle. They are worn with jodhpur boots and have a band at the bottom of each leg which you place under the instep of the boots. This keeps the pants legs from riding up on your leg. Kentucky jodhpurs are worn by saddle-seat riders in shows and are different from other jodhpurs and breeches in that they have no pegs. They fit the leg snugly from thigh to ankle, then flare out in a slight bell shape. They, too, have a band which goes beneath the instep of the jodhpur boot.

These are the basic varieties of riding pants, and the hunter-seat rider must be sure to buy breeches—not either of the other two styles. But likely as not, an unknowing buyer will end up with dark brown riding breeches. Now, nothing's wrong with brown riding breeches and if you can afford two or more pairs of riding pants, go ahead and get them. They are excellent for riding with friends or in small country shows. But they aren't right for large, more formal shows. The really experienced hunter-seat rider wears canary breeches in such shows and, if you show regularly, you won't feel at ease unless you have a pair of canaries.

The same goes for boots. They shouldn't be brown unless you plan to purchase more than one pair. Girl's boots should have either plain tops or tops of black patent leather. Only boys' boots may have brown tops— or they may be plain black. However, all boots should be comfortable, snug and high in the leg. There's nothing more unsightly than a rider in a pair of ill-fitting boots—loose around the calf and short below the knee.

If you intend to have one riding jacket, make it a black one. If you want more than one, choose a con-

Here you see how ratcatcher shirt looks.
A stock may be worn instead of bow tie

These girls, schooling for the next show, find
riding in blue jeans is perfectly comfortable

This young master cuts a dapper figure
in proper hunting attire. He needs only a
blue ribbon to put him on top of world

Here is more formal saddle seat riding wear.
Jacket and jodhpurs are of same material.
Wisely chosen color will accent horse's coat

From left are: full bridle with the basic types of bit—snaffle (left) and curb; dee bit snaffle; and curb bit

servative tweed for your second, or a lightweight material for summer.

A ratcatcher shirt may sound like something the Pied Piper should have worn, but actually it's a very stylish shirt designed specifically for hunting. These shirts are available in a wide range of checks, plaids, and stripes. The only difference between a ratcatcher shirt and an ordinary man's shirt is that the ratcatcher has no collar that folds over. Its collar is simply a straight band of whatever material the shirt is made of. This little collar buttons at the throat, and over it you wear a bow tie which comes with the shirt and is of the same pattern—or you can wear a stock. A stock is a long strip of white material which you tie so that it looks something like an ascot from the front. It is a traditional part of correct hunting attire and was worn originally as a convenient way of carrying a bandage. If some injury occurred during the hunt, the rider simply removed his stock and used it for first aid. If you have a black jacket, a snowy white stock and ratcatcher go with it better than anything else.

Equipment for the saddle-seat rider has more color range or leeway to it, though the colors are still subdued and conservative. A rider should never wear floppy clothing or loud colors around a horse, for they are apt to cause him to shy. Another reason for subdued tones is that you want your horse to be admired—and, of course, your ability to ride him well—rather than your bright clothes.

Now, exactly what does a rider need to be properly dressed in a saddle-horse class? 1) Kentucky jodhpurs, preferably of gabardine, 2) a man's shirt and tie, 3) a jacket which either matches or looks very well with your jodhpurs, 4) jodhpur boots, 5) a saddle derby.

About the colors we mentioned before—your jodhpurs and jacket will probably be available in shades of beige, brown, navy, black or gray. Any of these is suitable and you should simply choose a color that goes well with the color of your horse.

Where do you get these supplies? If your home town hasn't a store which sells riding equipment, Miller, M. J. Knoud, and H. Kaufman & Sons

48

The horse's full bridle shows correct position of bits and fit of decorative brow band

Use colored brow bands only on saddle type horses

in New York City are three outfitters of horses and horsemen—and three of the finest horse-supply stores anywhere in this country. Each of these stores sells only the best quality materials and yet offers a wide price range.

What do you wear when you are riding informally—hacking on the trails with friends, or working out in the ring? Saddle-seat riders will be most comfortable in inexpensive jodhpurs and jodhpur boots, while hunter-seat riders will fare best in breeches and boots. And in spite of what perfectionists say, I've never found any objection to wearing blue jeans and sturdy shoes. Go ahead and wear them if you don't find them uncomfortable.

But now let's figure out what you

need for your horse. The most obvious things are the bridle and saddle. These are referred to as 'tack.' To tack up a horse is to put his bridle and saddle on him, and the place where you keep the bridle, saddle and other stable supplies is called a tack room.

A saddle is fairly easy for you to select. You are the one who is best able to tell whether or not it is comfortable to ride in. If you're buying the saddle for a Saddle Horse, the horse should be round enough in the barrel (see chart on p. 10) so that the pommel of the saddle won't rub his withers. A hunter or jumper, on the other hand, is apt to be a rangy animal with more prominent withers than a gaited horse. Use a good sheepskin pad under the saddle to give protection and choose a saddle with a reasonably high pommel. Chances are that the saddle will fit the horse perfectly and the thing to be concerned with is whether it fits you.

A hunter-seat rider who is likely to do some jumping should pick a saddle with knee rolls (see the illustration on p. 46), and the girth should be of leather. The saddle-seat rider should

49

"S" shaped bit used on Walking horses

choose a saddle with straight flaps and a cloth girth because cloth is more decorative than plain leather. If you find the saddle comfortable when you ride or sit on it and if it looks about right for your horse, there's no more testing or searching to be done. Buy it.

Unfortunately, a good saddle is very expensive. The very least you will pay for a new saddle is about $50, but really good saddles sell for $200 to $400, so you may have to forget about buying a new one. Saddles are not expensive without a reason—they are crafted to last. You can pick up a fine used saddle for $100 to $200 and it will serve your purposes perfectly if you take the same care in fitting it to horse and rider as you would in making a new purchase. A used saddle will look well enough for showing and will be rugged enough to take the everyday wear you'll give it.

Bridles are a little more difficult to choose because you may not know exactly what bit is the correct one for your horse. You can get sound advice about selecting the proper bit from the former owner of your animal, or you might turn the question over to an experienced friend who has ridden your horse. Here are some pointers about the general type of bridle you will need, depending on the kind of horse you have bought.

Almost all Saddle Horses require a full bridle for maximum control, so if you own a three-gaited or five-gaited horse, always use the full bridle (see p. 49 for the illustration) on him. And remember to keep the snaffle bit *behind* the curb (as shown) when you bridle your horse.

The same general rule holds true for Walking Horses. Every Walking Horse should be shown with some version of the bit indicated in our illustration—the special walking-horse bit. Arabians and Morgans are also shown with consistently similar bridles—generally a Pelham bitted bridle (see illustration) or a full bridle.

All these breeds and types of horse should have decorative nose and brow bands when being ridden in a show, and none should ever be ridden with a martingale (shown on p. 51). Why? Because a martingale is designed as a restraint. It prevents a horse from tossing his head around. Now, since all the horses we have discussed should be well mannered as well as showy in action and appearance, using

A running martingale travels along reins

Rubber pelham is a good bit for hunters

a martingale would indicate that the horse is not always mannerly and would automatically eliminate him in any competition. Martingales should be used only on hunters and open jumpers—and then only when absolutely necessary. A running martingale, rather than a standing martingale, is your best bet because it controls the horse only when the reins are tight, allowing him freedom to maneuver in case of a fall or a difficult jump when your reins would be loose.

If you own a hunter or jumper, your choice of bit should depend entirely on how hard a mouth the horse has. If your horse responds well to the use of your hands and doesn't show much tendency to pull, use a mild bit—a 'snaffle' (see illustration p. 48). But if you feel you need firmer control, try a rubber Pelham. Should the horse's mouth be tougher, a full bridle ought to fill the bill.

Unlike saddles, new bridles are not prohibitive. A good full bridle for a three- or five-gaited horse can be bought at Miller's for under $60. You can get a new Walking-Horse bridle for under $50. A good snaffle bridle costs about $35, and a full snaffle-and-curb bridle begins at about $30. But if you must watch your expenses, you can buy a good used bridle for between $15 and $25.

You know now about the most important equipment you'll need. Of course, there are a number of little things you ought to have on hand around your stable so that you can

If you must lead horse without halter, loop belt around his neck or try method at right. Below trainer wraps twitch around horse's upper lip to distract him while medicine is applied

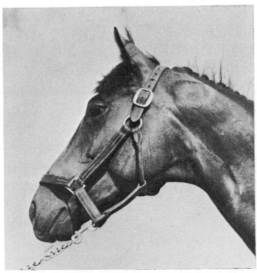

For safety's sake, keep a halter on your horse at all times and have spare handy

take proper care of your horse, either at home or at a show. Here is a list of items for you to think about getting and a few suggestions as to their use. Under the grouping of medicines, you won't find comments about usage because this information either will be on the container or will be discussed in a later chapter.

STABLE EQUIPMENT

Buckets—for watering the horse, cleaning tack, and general use around the stable.

Halters—two, one kept as a spare, and they should be of leather. Always keep your horse haltered so you can catch

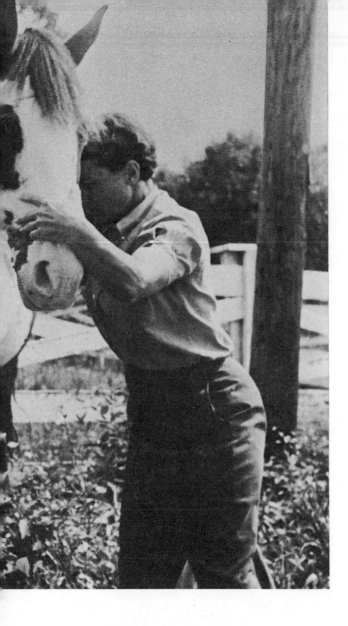

him in case of fire, accident, or any other emergency.

Lead shank—this should be of leather and chain, and kept in a convenient spot so you can find it readily.

Twitch— this consists of a strong length of wood, about half as long as a baseball bat. A small loop of rope or chain extends from a hole at one end of the wood. This loop is put over the horse's upper lip and twisted rather tight. It is used to restrain the horse and divert his attention when he is being shod, clipped, worked on by a doctor, or treated in some manner that would make the horse nervous.

Pitchfork—to fork hay at feeding time and to remove bedding from stall for replacement with fresh bedding.

Shovel—to be used for removing manure from the horse's stall.

Wheelbarrow— to remove manure from the barn.

Canvas webbing or *stall guard*—to place across the entrance of the horse's stall during the summer so the door can be left open.

A longe line—a length of canvas line with a chain end to be used for exercising the horse.

GROOMING EQUIPMENT

Curry comb, body brush, 'dandy' brush, hoof pick, mane comb—all to be used in cleaning the horse.

Clippers—to keep the horse's whiskers and fetlocks trimmed off, the mane and tail clipped on three-gaited horses, and to remove hair so medicines can be applied to possible sores.

MEDICAL EQUIPMENT

Alcohol	*Bandages*
Absorbent cotton	*Sheet cotton*
Tincture of iodine	*Mineral oil*
Colic mixture	*Linament*
Cough mixture	*Thrush medicine*
Kidney mixture	*Dose syringe*
Healing powder	*Yellow oxide of*
Gall lotion	*mercury*

None of these things is expensive and you don't need them all at once. Buy them when it's easy and convenient for you to do so and know, once you have them, that you have a well-equipped stable—prepared for everyday work and for most emergencies.

5

CARE AND FEEDING

Your horse spends more time in his stable than you do in your house. You can come and go as you please, but your horse can leave the barn only when you choose to take him out. That is why proper care for him starts with the stable in which he's kept.

Always be sure that there is good drainage away from the barn so that when it rains there is no seepage or dampness collecting in the stable. If a stable is to be built especially for your horse, remember to have it constructed so that the doorways face toward the south, leaving the north side of the barn a solid wall. This prevents cold winter winds from chilling the horse and allows you to keep the stable door open even during the colder months without his being in a

direct draft. A horse needs plenty of fresh air, so chances are that you need not worry about his being too cold. Unless you live in a region where the temperature drops way below freezing, you can leave the barn door partly open even during the winter. His winter coat will protect him, and he'll certainly be plenty warm enough if you put a blanket on him just as an extra precaution.

For added ventilation you may want your horse to have a window in his stall. If so, be sure the hinges are on the bottom of the window so that the top opens out into the stall. This forces the air to go up instead of directly onto the horse, and it keeps him from being exposed to a draft.

When summer comes, your horse

can have the full advantage of those mild summer breezes if you leave his stall door open and put canvas webbing, called a stall guard, across the doorway. This gives him fresh air yet keeps him securely in his home.

The stall itself ought to be a box stall—called that simply because it has the shape of a square box—no smaller than 10 by 10 feet. Ideally, the floor of the stall should be of clay and around the inside perimeter planks should be laid—not nailed down—so as to prevent their becom-

ing warped and allow you to clean under them once in a while. However, if the entire stall is planked, the boards should be placed very tightly together so your horse won't catch a shoe and possibly twist his leg. And before you put your horse in his stall for the night, always be certain to check its condition. A dog or rabbit may have gotten inside and could scare your horse badly in the dark. Remember—whenever a horse is in danger of being frightened, he is also in danger of being injured.

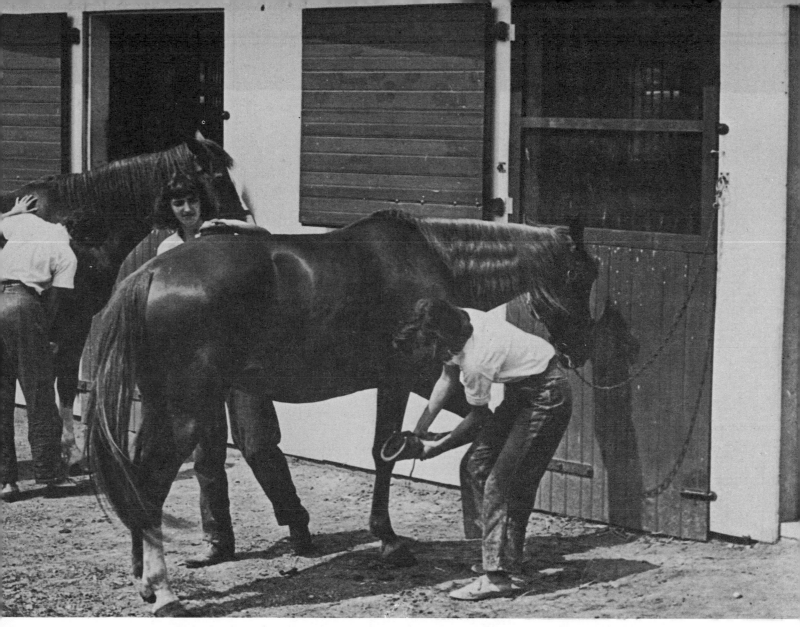

Spit and polish pay off in glossy coats, gleaming hoofs, and tangle-free manes and tails

The passageways or aisles of a stable are safest when they are made simply of dirt, raked and leveled often. Of course, concrete or wood planking is also used. But concrete is very slippery and should be roughened if a horse is to walk on it without risking injury.

Your stable, in order to be complete, needs a tack room—an area set aside for the bridle, saddle, blankets, medicines and other equipment. It need not be large but everything should have its place, and all articles should be stored so that you can find them at night with a flashlight.

Just as exercise is important, to your health and growth, so it is important to the development of your horse. That's why you will want to have a paddock handy—a dry, level, fenced-in area where you can let your horse have a good workout. After all, there may be days when you won't be able to go for a ride. On those occasions, you should either longe your horse or simply turn him loose and let him romp around in the paddock for the afternoon.

To longe a horse, take the chain end (if your longe line doesn't have a chain, then take the end with the snap clasp on it) and run it through the brass ring on one side of the horse's halter, over his nose, and attach the snap to the brass ring on the other side of his halter. Lead the horse to the paddock, being sure to take a carriage whip or longe whip with you. Stand in the center of the paddock and slowly let out the longe line while you use the whip merely to shoo the horse away from you. Soon he will be making a circle around you, and when the line is fully extended, the horse will be able to trot and canter briskly while you do nothing more than stand in the center holding the line. And remember that you should change directions now and then so that the horse won't get dizzy or become sore in one shoulder.

After the horse has been ridden or longed, or become hot from racing around on his own, take care to cool him off properly before putting him back in his stall. Cooling a horse after exercising him is one of the truly vital aspects of caring for a horse (see p. 62). If you put the animal away while he's hot or even let him stand still when he's hot, you'll probably give your poor horse a good case of founder, or laminitis (see Chapter 6). Or, if you let the horse eat or drink his fill of water before he has cooled down, the horse is likely to get a serious, even fatal, case of colic.

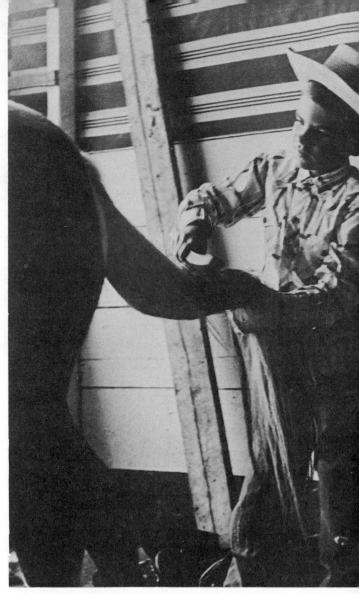

It takes patience to get out all the knots

The way to cool a horse in warm weather is to wash him down with warm water mixed with disinfectant. Use a sponge and rub him well, so that all the caked sweat is removed. Then, with a scraper remove the excess water from the horse's body and proceed to walk him until he's dry and cool, allowing him to stop every ten minutes or so for a few sips of water. Remember not to let him drink his fill, no matter how hard he strains at the shank.

Naturally, if the weather is bitter cold or even mildly chilly, you should not wash a horse down when he's hot. If he gets sweated up in cool weather, simply go over him with a slightly damp sponge. Then put a blanket or a shaped blanket cover called a 'cooler' over him and walk him, again permitting the horse to have a couple of sips of water ever so often.

To groom your horse well, you need a currycomb (a hard rubber comb is best), a 'dandy' (stiff) brush, a body brush, and a rub rag, mane comb and hoof pick. First, use the dandy brush to clean off the horse's face and head. Then, using brisk circular motions, apply the currycomb to the horse's neck and body—but not to the lower legs. After the horse has been thoroughly curried, use the dandy brush again to whisk away the dirt you have removed from the horse's skin. Also use this brush to clean off the animal's lower legs. Then take the softer body brush and go over the horse once more to bring out the shine in his coat.

Next, you should comb out the horse's mane with the mane comb. Don't worry about hurting him; there are no nerve endings in the roots of the mane hair, so you can pull as hard as you have to. Comb the tail with your fingers only. Be sure to clean out your horse's hooves. Take the hoof pick and, with your back toward the horse's head so you face the rear, pick up each hoof, place it between your knees and remove all dirt packed in the hoof.

Now you are virtually finished with the grooming of your horse. All that remains is to give him a final once-over with the rub rag. This will bring added gloss to his coat and give him a feeling of life and vigor.

As for feeding a horse—well, there's more to it than meets the eye. There are many different grades of feed and you'll want to be sure your horse is getting what's good for him. Oats are the main ingredient in any mixture, and they are the best supplement to hay. Good quality oats should weigh about forty pounds or more per bushel and should have a good bright color to them. The grains should be dry and brittle, never soggy.

Crushed oats are actually better for horses than whole oats—especially young horses. However, once oats have been crushed, you have no way of telling whether they are of good or poor quality. So the safest thing to do is to buy an oat crusher and crush your own whole oats. Crushed oats take up more bulk than whole oats, so the number of quarts you must give your horse differs. The average working sixteen-hand horse should have between eight and twelve quarts of crushed oats—fed twice a day.

Remember, there isn't a great variety of things for your horse to eat and so, to prevent him from becoming bored with his food, you should see that he occasionally gets a taste of grains other than oats. Bran is one of the grains that he may have. Actually, the outer covering of *any* grain is called bran, but the best for horses is wheat bran. Its value is that it produces a healthy, mild, laxative effect. You should mix about a quart of bran in with your horse's oats (that is, replace a quart of oats with a quart of bran) two or three times a week. Add hot water to this mixture and allow it to stand for about ten minutes before presenting your pet with a tasty damp mash.

Another food frequently given to horses is corn. It is rich in vitamin A and especially good for horses in winter because it produces body heat. When you feed your horse corn, be sure to give him corn on the cob instead of cracked corn. Cracked corn, if it is left to stand for a long time, loses its food value and turns rancid. Corn on the cob also gives your horse something to do during the lonely hours when you aren't with him. But make sure the cobs are large so there's no danger of the horse's choking. The best routine is to give the horse two ears of corn at night when there's nothing going on to excite him and he can munch them to his heart's content.

Barley and flaxseed are other supplements to a horse's basic grain—oats. But these should be used sparingly: only about a handful of each mixed with the rest of the feed in a cooked mash.

All horses find molasses very tasty and it's also high in food value. So if your horse is a finicky eater or if you just want to give him a treat, mix in some cane molasses with his feed.

Now, there are a number of conflicting ideas on what type of manger should be used for feeding a horse. A manger is a large, sturdy bowl-like thing in which the horse's food is put. Many stables are equipped with iron mangers fitted into the corner of the stall. Other horsemen use wooden mangers, while still others maintain that a horse's feed should be placed on the floor because this allows him to stretch his neck and because eating from the ground is a horse's natural feeding position. The big fault with this last system is that worm eggs often collect on a stable floor, and if a horse is forced to nibble his food from the ground, he's likely to pick up some of the eggs.

The problem with a permanent manger—of wood or iron—affixed to the stall itself is that it is one more object on which a nervous horse can injure himself. Such dangers are the reason why many horsemen suggest the use of a relatively new type of manger which is made of rubber and can be removed from the stall when the horse has finished eating.

As we said earlier, grain is what gives a horse energy. But his real staff of life is hay, which consists of long grasses mown and dried. A horse can survive without grain but not without hay, and a horse will overeat grain but not hay. In fact, your horse should have hay in front of him at all times. Of course, this does not mean that you should overfeed him. Three good pitchforks full of hay should last him from one feeding to the next, and he should leave no more than about

Young Thoroughbred gets exercise on longe line. Whip is to keep him at brisk gait and moving in smooth circle

half a forkful uneaten.

The best kind of hay to feed your horse consists of timothy mixed with alfalfa and clover. You can tell a good bale of hay the moment it's tossed down from the hayloft. When it lands on the ground, it should be springy and bouncy; it shouldn't hit the ground like a sack of cement. When the bale is opened, the hay should have a fresh, grassy smell; it should not be moldy or musty. You can identify mold in hay easily because it has a distinctive gray color and looks a bit like frost.

Again, some people feed a horse his hay in an iron manger—called a hayrack—attached to the wall of the stall, while others simply toss it on the ground in one corner.

Aside from hay, two other things should be in your horse's stall and available to him at all times: water, and a block of salt (iodized, if you live in a part of the country where there is insufficient iron in the earth).

If for any reason you do not keep water before your horse at all times and must take him out of his stall to water him at a trough, try to water him frequently. And be sure to water him before, not after, feeding him in the morning and at night.

At night you'll want your horse to have a dry, clean, fresh bed to lie on. The bedding he'll like best will be of wheat straw. Only straw is used in fine stables because it's the cleanest of all beddings. Furthermore, there's no danger of a horse eating his straw as long as he has hay in front of him. Of course, there are other beddings which are quite satisfactory. Peat moss, wood shavings and sawdust are all used, as well as pine needles, often found in southern stables. Because of its tar content, peat moss is especially good for horses with bad hooves. In the daytime, the bedding should be pitchforked out of the stall and allowed to dry in the sun so that the clean, dry parts can be re-used.

Now you are ready to give your horse the care he deserves. Make sure you have a good supply of feed and grain and bedding. Regular feeding is important to every horse and he must not be forced to go hungry because you have forgotten to check up on the food supply. And remember, a feed man isn't as readily available as the local delicatessen; it may be a matter of days before he can deliver your order. So always keep on the safe side and have plenty of food ready for the pet you love.

61

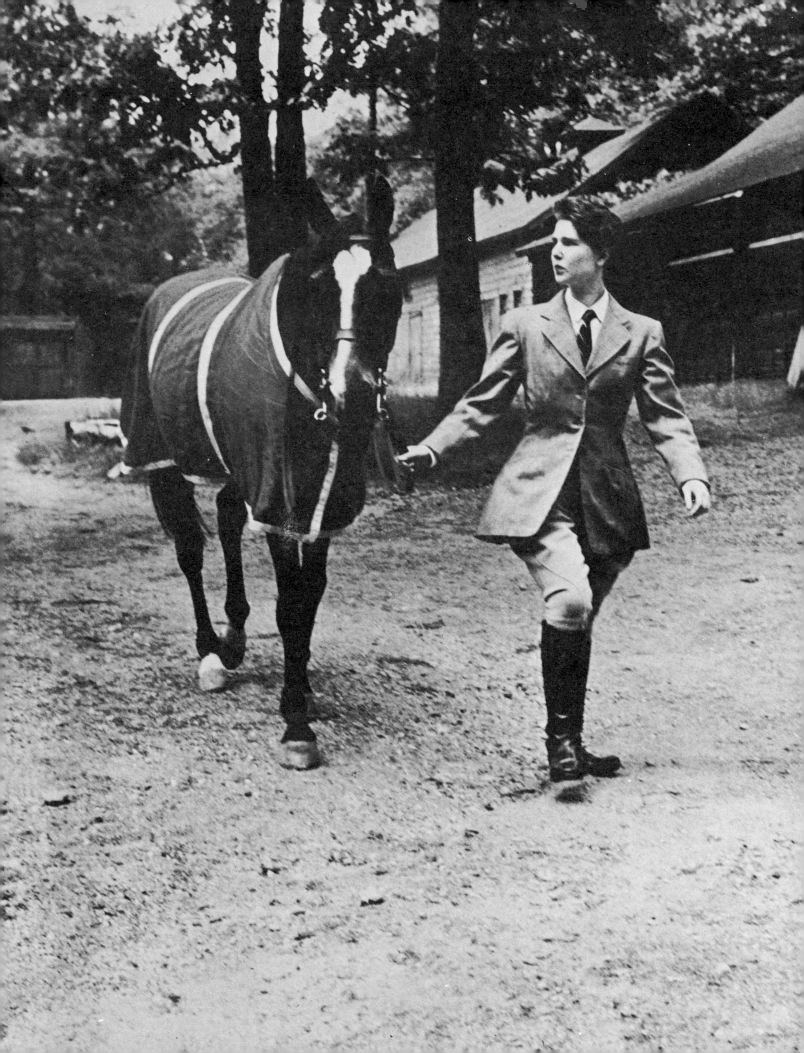

FIRST AID

6

Every day, accidents occur—sometime, somewhere. Most of us think of accidents as they affect people, but you must realize that accidents can happen to horses as well.

Illness strikes horses as well as it does human beings. A horse can get a cold just the same as you, and other sicknesses can plague him. The all-too-common horse complaints are colic, distemper, thrush, and lameness. Because they are so frequent, you must be prepared for these emergencies and know how to help your horse, or when to call a veterinarian (a doctor, you will remember, who treats animals; the word is often shortened to "vet").

But before we come to these problems, you must realize that there are two things even a healthy horse needs regularly—and these you cannot do for him. First, any horse that gets ridden will have to be shod about every six weeks. Make certain that you use a reputable blacksmith. He will know just what type of shoe to put on your horse. For example, if you own a pleasure hack, a hunter or a jumper, the best shoes will be light, flat ones. But a gaited horse will require weighted shoes so that he'll lift his feet high. In winter a horse may need leather pads on his front hooves to prevent the soles from becoming bruised—or corks to keep him from slipping.

The second thing your horse will need is to be wormed at least once a year by a veterinarian.

In Chapter 4, there was a list of medical supplies you ought to keep on hand in your tack room, preferably in some separate cabinet. Now you are going to see how to use some of those supplies.

Colic is one of the most frequent and one of the most painful sicknesses to strike a horse. Some kinds, according to Dr. Manuel Gilman, Examining Veterinarian of the New York State Race Tracks, are generally fatal and these require the expert attention of the vet. Other forms of it are serious but can be treated successfully by you.

Colic is a bad pain in the abdomen—the region just below the horse's stomach (see chart on p. 10). It causes more deaths among horses than any other single illness, death being due to failure of the horse's heart as a result of pressure from gasses. The causes of colic are, in the order of their frequency: bad feeding, over-feeding, feeding the horse when he is hot or excited, and poisonous weeds sometimes found in hay.

One type of colic is gas colic. This is not basically serious, but it can become so if not attended to promptly. A second type is called impaction colic. This occurs when a quantity of grain becomes stopped in the horse's intestine and prevents anything from moving. You should know that *a horse cannot vomit*. This means that if his digestive tract is blocked, he's in for real trouble. A third form of colic is sand colic. This is found primarily in the West, in regions where horses are on sparse pasture during droughts. The horse, in trying to get at the scrub grass, picks up sand. The sand accumulates and, in time, stops up the bowels.

When a horse has mild colic, the first thing he will do is stop eating. Then you'll begin to notice that he looks around at his abdomen. Frequently he will lie down and roll, and his eyes will have a staring expression. He may break out in a sweat.

If the horse has severe colic, you'll have no trouble recognizing it. He will roll violently and thrash his feet about. He'll be wet with sweat and his eyes will be noticeably bloodshot. You will have to hit him to get him to his feet and, once he's up, you will have trouble keeping him on all fours.

When you find that your horse has severe colic, call a vet immediately. Then follow the instructions for treating mild colic while you wait for the vet to arrive.

In cases of mild colic, the first thing to do is to remove the feed and water from the horse's stall. Then put a shank on the horse and, if he's lying down, firmly get him to his feet and walk him. Give him some colic mixture with a dose syringe according to the directions on the bottle. You will need help from one of your parents or from a friend. This person should hold your horse and quiet him while you are busy giving him his medicine. After the colic mixture, you should give him four (4) or five (5) ounces of warm water with the syringe by mouth (see p. 65) to wash away the irritating taste of the medicine, followed by the same amount of mineral oil, also given with a dose syringe by mouth. When you are not giving the horse medicine, keep him walking. Remember, your horse's life may be at stake.

When you are pretty sure that your pet has only mild colic, wait an hour after treating him before you call the veterinarian. If after an hour, however, he seems no better, then be sure you get a doctor for your horse.

Founder (or laminitis) is another ailment common to horses. Founder is actually a serious congestion of the blood vessels inside the horse's hooves,

Stones in horse's shoe cause lameness

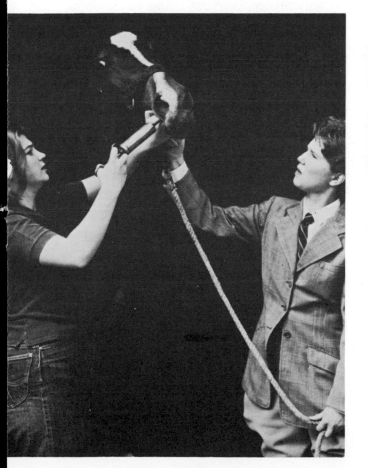

At left, horse gets medicine by syringe correctly placed through side of mouth. This forces liquid down throat. Wrong way, above, is through front of mouth. 65

and it usually affects both front feet. It can be caused by a number of things such as toxins or poisons, accumulated from poor shoeing or concussion on hard roads, and mares can get founder from carrying heavy foals. Founder can also result from a horse's having had colic. However, the commonest cause is allowing a horse to stand still for more than a few minutes after he has had heavy exercise. That is why it is essential for you to walk your horse whenever he gets hot before you put him back in his stall.

The symptoms of founder are unmistakeable—the horse simply does not want to move and, in many cases, really cannot move. If your horse does walk, he will move gingerly, as though he were walking on eggs. Also, he will run a temperature: you will be able to feel fever in his front hooves. A horse's normal temperature, taken by rectum, is 99° to 100½° Fahrenheit. When he has founder, he will run a temperature of about 102° or even higher. (To take his temperature, you will again need help. Have the horse's head held steady while you insert the thermometer, heavily coated with Vaseline, into the rectal opening. Stand well to the side of the haunch so that he cannot kick out at you. You should hold the thermometer in place about three (3) or four (4) minutes—the time you would need with a child.)

When the case of founder is severe, the animal will break out into a sweat and may even refuse to stand up. You

Bandage is tied on by strings at end. To re-roll bandage, start from string end

should remove the horse's shoes as gently as you can, and get a veterinarian to look at him as soon as possible. The longer you wait, the less chance there is for recovery. If no vet is available, the first thing you should do is to stop feeding your horse corn and give him bran mash instead, at both feedings. Now prepare for the real treatment. Get some epsom salts and put a good double handful in a pail of hot water. Soak the horse's hooves for an hour in this mixture, then apply crushed ice packs. Alternate the procedure every hour.

If you can clear up the condition with one day—or a day and a half, at the most—recovery will be complete. But if the sickness persists for two or three days, you may have a chronic cripple on your hands.

Coughs and colds are usually associated with young horses and, as in the case of humans, they are generally caused by a virus type of infection for which there is no quickly effective treatment. As long as your horse has a simple cold, then, there is no need to call in a vet. The horse's cold will last for about ten days to two weeks, unless complications set in. During that time, you should keep your horse in his stall and blanket him. Feed him a bran mash once a day (he can have his usual mixture for his second meal) and take his temperature at least twice a day. A horse's cold, like the cold you may get, is catching, so you should keep him away from other horses. And just as you do when you have a cold, your horse may have a runny nose. If so, the best thing is to put a little Vicks salve in each nostril (see p. 65).

Should complications set in, however, your horse may be in danger of getting pneumonia. When a cold becomes severe, the horse will run a high fever and will not eat. If this happens, your pet needs antibiotics, like the ones you are sometimes given for a hard cold, and he needs the care of a vet. Call your vet as soon as you find out, by taking the horse's temperature, that the fever has gotten out of hand. Over 102° is a sure danger signal.

Thrush is a disease that affects horses' hooves. It is the rotting of the 'frog' (that small horn of hoof-flesh shaped like triangle, with its base at the back of the horse's hoof where the horseshoe is open) and is caused by poor sanitation, or lack of proper hygiene. That is why it is important to keep your pet's stall clean and to use the hoof pick often to make sure his hooves are in good condition.

If your horse has thrush, you will notice, first of all, that there is a nasty odor coming from his hooves. On inspecting them, you'll see that there is a definite softening of the frog. The rotted area should be cut out carefully by your blacksmith, and you should apply thrush medicine as directed on the container to cure him of this unpleasant disease.

Lameness can be caused by both thrush and founder, so if you discover that your horse is lame, check to see if either of these diseases is at the root of the problem.

To find out if your horse is lame, trot him a few yards and watch his feet and legs. The leg which the horse favors and puts the least weight on is the lame one. If the horse is lame in one of his front legs, he will nod or duck his head when the sound, or healthy, foot touches the ground. If he is lame in a rear leg, he will nod when the lame foot hits the ground.

Now, assuming that you've looked to see if your horse has laminitis or thrush and that you've found he has neither of these, the next thing you must do is to see whether he has a stone in one hoof—or perhaps even nails or a piece of glass. If he does, remove the matter with your hoof pick and then apply a poultice, or wet bandage, to the hoof. This means simply that you wrap the hoof in a clean, heavy bandage and keep it damp with water. Also feel the hoof

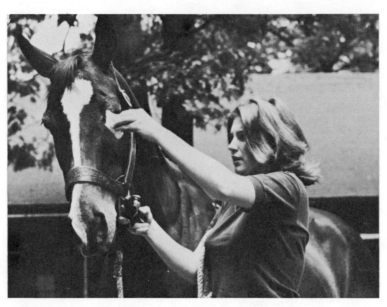

Yellow oxide of mercury will clear up weepiness caused by a minor infection

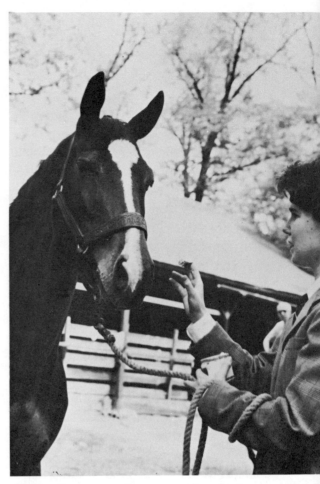

Alpha Queen warily eyes salve to be applied to nostrils for a runny nose

to see if it is very hot. If so, apply poultices until the fever goes down.

If the horse's lameness does not seem to be caused by some trouble with his hoof, then feel along the horse's leg to see if he has a fevered ankle or tendon. If you feel heat in the horse's leg, apply a poultice to that area and bind it on (see p. 66), being sure to wrap the bandage tight enough to hold the poultice in place but not so tight as to stop circulation to the foot and lower leg. If, within two days, the condition does not improve, call your veterinarian.

Lameness may be caused by a misplaced nail in the shoe. If your horse has been shod within three days before becoming lame, you'll do well to remove the shoe on the lame leg.

Sometimes you may find that your horse has an eye that is weepy, or an eyelid that is swollen or half-closed. This condition may be caused by a temporary infection, in which case all you need do is apply yellow oxide of mercury around the eye (see p. 68) and the condition should clear up. If after four or five days your horse still has a running eye, you should get the veterinarian to take a look at him.

Strangles, or distemper, is a highly contagious illness which affects the horse's throat. It usually occurs when a Western horse is brought into the barn. Western horses are more frequently exposed to streptococcus (a form of bacteria which causes the sickness) because they are not stabled and eat rough grasses on the open range. Should your horse catch strangles, he will not eat and—in fact—will barely be able to swallow. He will run a high temperature, have swellings in his throat area, and will have a discharge of puss from the nostrils.

This disease can be fatal and it can also cause permanent damage to your horse's respiratory (or breathing) system, so, as soon as you discover that your horse has strangles, alert the doctor. Keep the horse completely isolated—in quarantine—from other horses all during his illness and for two weeks after the last symptoms have disappeared.

Let us suppose that your horse may have cut himself or gotten some sort of surface wound. You should wash the wound in soap and warm water, dry the wound gently and apply gall lotion or sulpha powder to the cut. If possible, the wound should be bandaged with gauze, then wrapped in an outer bandage and dressed (or changed) daily.

However, if the wound is a puncture type of wound—say, from a nail—and not simply a surface wound, you should have the vet give your pet a tetanus shot. Your doctor will then tell you how best to handle the treatment of the particular wound.

Now you know a little about some of the commoner illnesses that strike horses and what to do if your horse is hurt or falls sick. This chapter gives you no more than necessary First Aid information. The important thing to remember is that the best care for a sick horse is trained care. That is why you must never hesitate to call the vet if you find your horse is ill and you are not sure of just what the trouble is. Always remember that, if your horse becomes sick, *you* are the one who has to take charge until the vet arrives. Your horse is like a big baby: he will be frightened and may resist treatment. If you have to be stern, if you have to use a twitch (see p. 52) to make the horse stand still, or hit him to get him up in case of colic, don't be afraid to do so. In the end, both you and your horse will be glad you took whatever measures were needed to insure his recovery.

Keep in mind at all times that your horse's life is actually in your hands. It is up to you to see that he does not overeat and become sick from colic. It is up to you to see that, when you exercise your horse, you use good judgment, common sense and kindness. A horse will run himself literally into the ground if you ask him to. He may not stop until he falls dead from exhaustion. So be sure to give him rest periods when you exercise him. The best rule to follow when you ride a horse is to walk him the first fifteen minutes after leaving the barn and the last fifteen minutes before returning to it. If you give a little thought to your pet's welfare, you'll have a long, happy life together.

69

7

COMMON SENSE OF RIDING

You've got your horse and all your equipment, and you're pretty sure you know how to care for him so that he'll live to the age of thirty. Now nature has provided you with a brisk, clear day, and you can't wait to mount up and go for the first real ride since you've owned your own horse.

If you are an experienced rider, there's nothing to prevent you from mounting up and riding off. But if you are a beginner, be prudent about this first adventure. First of all, your parents may be watching and you certainly won't want to make some silly, avoidable mistake in front of them or anyone else on your maiden voyage. Second, it's one thing to feed and care for a horse and keep him healthy; you're on solid ground there,

and if you are puzzled about something, you can always ask a friend or check it in the book. But it's a totally different thing when you're five or six feet off the ground on an animal which is a lot stronger than you! Third, and most important, you have your own sense of pride and responsibility. You must honestly estimate how well you ride and just how far you are able to go in terms of your own horsemanship. Learn thoroughly each step involved in riding before you advance to the next step. Never try to show off or be a daredevil—not only because that sort of behavior is childish but because it is dangerous and indicates that you simply aren't ready to have a horse of your own.

Of course, you never intentionally

71

do something foolish on a horse. But riding fills a person with a feeling of carefree ease, of delight and exuberance. It is very easy to get carried away and try something, such as jumping, which looks like so much fun but which you may not be ready to begin. So keep a level head and don't go overboard out of excitement.

But now it's time to mount up. Be sure you do it from the left side. Lead the horse from the barn and stand him in a quiet spot away from any other activity. Turn your back toward the horse's head so that you are facing toward the rear. With your left hand gather your reins (see p. 72) and hold the pommel of the saddle. With your right hand hold the stirrup (on the horse's left side)

and place your left foot in it. Now move your right hand to the cantle (that is the rear part of the saddle) and pull yourself up as you push off the ground with your right foot. Once your weight is firmly on your left foot in the stirrup, swing your right leg over the rear of the horse and gently sit down in the saddle, placing your right foot in the right stirrup. Do remember to land gently, though, and not to flop down on the horse's tender loins like a sack of meal!

To dismount, you reverse the procedure. Take your right foot out of the stirrup, swing it over the rear of the horse so that you are standing on your left foot, which is in the stirrup. Lean your body over the saddle so you can kick your left foot out of

Mounting: gather reins in left hand and place left foot in stirrup. Hold pommel of saddle and cantle (rear)

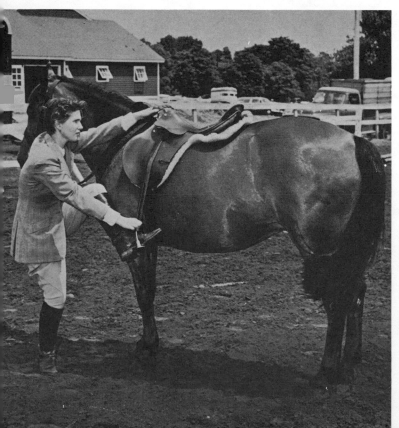
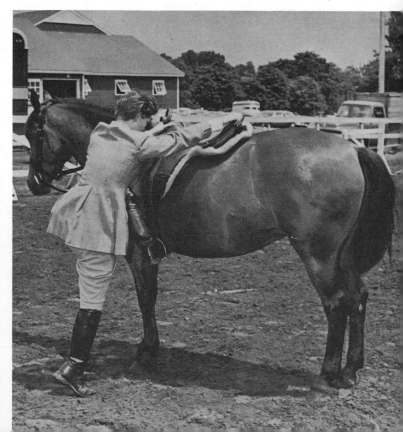

the stirrup. Then jump down.

Once you are on the horse, you must be certain that your stirrups are properly adjusted. The length of the stirrups will vary according to the type of riding you will be doing. The person who intends to do some jumping would wear his stirrups somewhat shorter than the person who rides saddle seat. But if you are simply going out for a pleasure ride (called hacking), the best way to adjust your stirrups is to let your legs hang relaxed as you sit in the saddle. Then fix your stirrup length so that the bottom of the iron comes to your ankle bone. This is a good average length and you can always raise or lower the stirrup a notch to suit your needs. But make sure that your stir-rups are even; otherwise, you'll be riding lopsided.

At last you're in the saddle and all set to go. But question yourself once more: are you *sure* you're ready to ride? Are you in the correct position, with every part of you poised exactly as it should be and set to stay that way? Your head and shoulders should be erect but not stiff. Your back should be straight, never sloppily hunched over. Your weight should be forward in the saddle and forward in your body—resting on your pelvic bones, *not* on the coccyx, the base of your spine. Your knees and legs are your means of hanging on in case the horse shies or bucks, so they should grip the saddle tight at all times. Never allow daylight to peek through

to pull up as you push off ground with right foot. Swing right leg over horse's back and sit down easily

A good fit and protection for your head

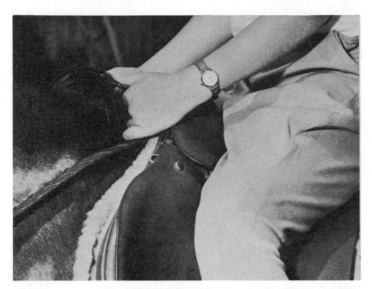

Snaffle bridle has one rein. Here we see the way to hold it, with hands well down

between your knees and the saddle, and if you want to test yourself on your ability to keep your knees in tight, try riding with a coin between them and the saddle. If the coin slips to the ground, you will know that you need to work harder.

Your heels must always be down and your toes should point forward as they would in your own natural walking position. Your ankles should be flexed slightly outward forcing your knees in and your feet away from the horse's sides. The stirrup should be right on the ball of the foot, and your heel well down.

As for your hands, make sure, first of all, that you are holding the reins correctly and that you have light contact with the horse's mouth. You should not pull at his mouth, but there

should be no slack in the reins except for the curb rein, the bottom rein. This should always be a little loose. Your thumbs should not be straight up nor should your hands be held in a completely horizontal position—as if you were suddenly going to start playing a piano! Instead, your hands should be midway between those two positions (see p. 75). In fact, the best way to get the proper angle is to rest your hands, while holding the reins, against the horse's shoulders on either side of his withers. The natural angle of his shoulders is the natural angle for your hands.

How high ought your hands to be held? About an inch or two over the horse's withers. And remember not to let those hands go flying up in the air in a moment of excitement! As for holding on to the saddle—that's a real crime for anyone but the extreme beginner who may need to steady himself now and then.

Also, remember to keep your elbows in close to your body. Let's not have any wings flapping out at the sides as if you were a huge bird ready to rise in flight!

Bear in mind that riding a horse is not merely sport, a question of strength or athletic ability. Truly, it is an art that has a lot in common with dancing; as you progress, you will gain a sense of balance and rhythm

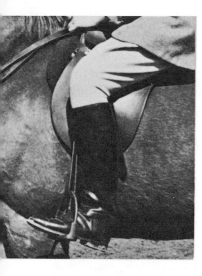

At left, correct way to hold two reins. The upper or snaffle rein is outside the little finger

At far left, the rider has feet too far forward. Toe and knee should form a straight line

Below, beginner pays close attention as instructor gives him pointers

that a dancer might well envy. And when you sit your horse, you will come to feel you are working with a partner. Every natural action of the horse is based on a distinct beat, so you must be as close to your horse as possible. Your thighs and calves must be held in tight, your hands close to his neck, your elbows near your sides. No part of you should flail out. Keep your senses tuned to the horse's movements and soon your own responses will become completely graceful and natural.

Now it's time to get on the move. To make the horse walk forward, simply kick him with your heels by moving the leg back from the knee and tapping the horse in the ribs. Don't lift up your whole leg from the thigh and dig the poor animal in an ungainly fashion, and above all don't jiggle the reins and expect the horse to know what it is that you want him to do.

The reins are for stopping and turning the horse. If you want to stop him, pull back steadily and evenly on the reins. Just pull by flexing your wrists. Don't lean back in the saddle and tug with all your might, nor should you jerk or snatch at the reins. A little movement from the wrists is all it takes, and after a few steps the average horse will stop. Horses with superior training will stop on a dime at the slightest touch from the hands or will increase their gait at the barest shift in the rider's weight.

The horse is now moving at a nice

walk and you know how to stop him. Fine. The only trouble is, what good is it to know how to stop and start the horse if you can't steer him? He'll have enough sense not to run into anything, but he may well carry you right into the nearest grain bin or pile of hay! To turn the horse and make him go where you want him to go, pull evenly and firmly on the rein near the direction you want to have him head. In other words, if you want to go right, pull steadily on the right rein—pull it straight back to your body, not out to the side. To go to the left, pull on the left rein.

There are some horses—such as Western horses or polo ponies—which are 'bridle wise' and steer in a different fashion because they must be ridden with one hand. If you know your horse is bridle wise and you want to turn left, lean the right rein against the right side of his neck. If you want to turn right, push the left rein against the left side of his neck. Instead of pulling your horse's head toward the direction you want to go, you push his head in that direction.

Aside from these basic details, there are certain fundamentals of riding you should be aware of before taking your first trip out on your horse. A chief rule is that you should never blame the horse for anything that happens while you are riding. If the horse shies at something which frightens him and you fall off, don't say "he threw me" and decide that the horse is at fault. It's up to you to

Even top riders take a spill so don't feel it is anything to be ashamed or badly frightened of

Hunters and riders near "in" gate awaiting their turn in the ring. Nervous horses are kept walking. Calmer ones stand quietly

Schedules for classes and diagrams of courses are posted near "in" gate. Here information gets a final check before the next class begins

77

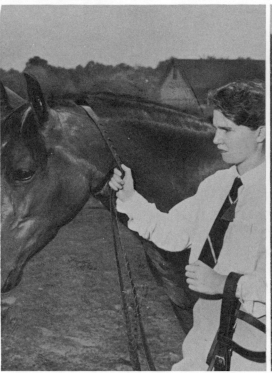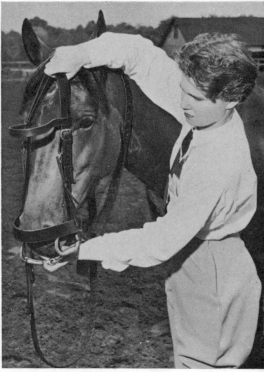

To bridle horse, loop reins over neck so he can't walk off; then slip bridle on

anticipate when a horse might become scared by something strange. You must be alert enough to feel the horse tense up, and you must be ready to soothe your pet and grip your knees in tight so that, if he does shy, you're ready. The sure sign of a poor rider is a person's saying that the horse threw him rather than admitting that he fell off.

Always bear in mind that you must have respect for your own horse and for other riders. Don't work your horse hard without giving him rest periods. He must surely be walked the first and last fifteen minutes of a ride and should never be ridden at more than a walk on hard roads. Why? Remember about laminitis? Your horse is likely to get it if you trot or canter him on pavement or before the circulation in his feet has had a chance to be stimulated by walking.

If you're riding on a bridle path and come upon other riders, assume that there may be a timid horse or a novice rider in the group and *walk* past these people instead of galloping by them. Suppose you were one of these riders and you had been on a horse only once or twice before. Some young rider comes galloping by, your horse takes off after him, you lose control and wind up taking an ugly fall. It's all quite avoidable if we observe common courtesy on the trails.

Speaking of falls, we might as well face the fact that some time during your career as a rider you are likely to take a spill. At the start, get all sorts of adventurous ideas about

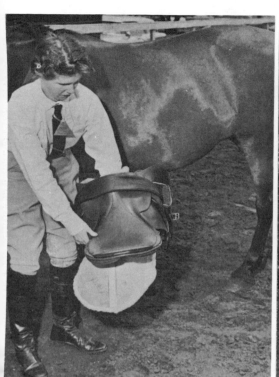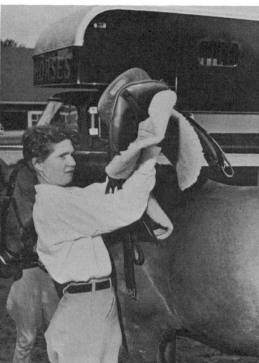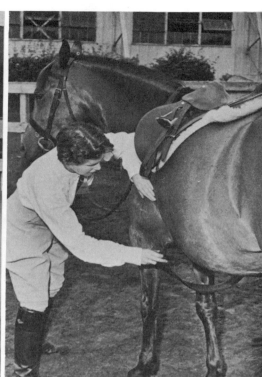

Pull up stirrups, lay girth across saddle before placing saddle pad and saddle, and fastening girth underneath

broken bones out of your mind. Riding a horse is no more dangerous than riding a bicycle, and a serious accident with a horse happens even less often than a serious accident with a bicycle. The only difference is that fewer people ride horses, so that when an accident occurs people remember it more clearly and make more of it. There's always somebody with a relative who was a victim of the classic equine tragedy—being dragged by a frightened horse, one foot caught in the stirrup. Granted, something like this does happen once in a while. However, many riders who have been riding for fifteen years or more and have seen a goodly number of spills, report never having seen anyone dragged or stepped on by a horse.

Now, if nothing can convince you

that fear of being dragged by a stirrup is unwarranted, you will feel a good deal safer if you use special stirrups with a safety bar. When the toe catches on this bar, the stirrup unhinges and releases the foot. These stirrups are never used in horse shows, however, and any rider who keeps his heels down firmly has no need of this type of stirrup iron.

But such incidents are truly freak. They never happen to a good rider or to a beginner on a suitable horse taking suitable precautions—and they happen only very rarely to other riders, even the most careless of them.

If you are still worried about falls, there are a few precautions you can take—and which every rider should know how to take—to make your rides as safe as possible. The most

79

THE CROWNING GLORY

8

But many months must inevitably pass between the time you first start practicing the elementary steps in riding and the time you are ready for a rider's dream come true—entering the big-time National Horse Show at Madison Square Garden, in New York City; the Grand National, in San Francisco; the Chicago International; The American Royal, in Kansas City, or the International, in Washington, D. C. During those months, or perhaps even years, of practice you should acquire three chief talents.

First of all, you should develop a feeling of true closeness and friendship with your horse. This means that you not only love him but understand him. You have some idea of what 'makes him tick.' You've ridden him so often that, nearly every time he makes a move, you know what to expect next. You know that if he lays his ears back while you're riding with other horses, he is likely to kick out because someone is riding too close to his heels. If you're riding along the trail and you feel him tense up, you will be aware of the fact that he might be frightened and about to shy at something. Perhaps you feel him grab at the bit and try to put his head down. Then you should know whether he's about to buck or whether he's merely making a stab at picking up some grass along the way. In short, you should become sensitive to his every mood. Then you will be able to tell if he's relaxed and gentle or if he's nervous and frisky. You are practically certain of just how far you can trust him—and you have a good idea of how far he trusts you.

Well, you might ask yourself, what has this feeling of "togetherness" got to do with Madison Square Garden, or the San Francisco Cow Palace? It has this to do with it: it means that when you enter the big ring with bright lights shining down on you and several thousand people concentrating on your performance, you aren't simply on any old animal hoping for the best—you are with a friend. The two of you are working as a team. You aren't two frightened strangers in the middle of an arena, each wondering what the other is going to do. And as soon as you enter that ring, you'll realize that the feeling of closeness, trust and friendship between you and your horse is not only wonderful in itself but is a tremendous advantage in a show. You are far luckier than the rider who sees his mount an hour or so a day and who has a groom to take care of such things as cleaning and feeding him. In such cases, the horse becomes a friend of the groom—not the rider.

The second quality you'll develop is a sense of balance. No one can teach you this. It comes about with constant practice, with hours of riding day after day. Soon it becomes automatic. You move right with the horse without even thinking about it. You develop ease and flexibility in every action while you're mounted, and you stay on the horse with scarcely any concentration at all on keeping those knees in, and heels and hands down.

The third skill you must develop is an ability to perform certain technical exercises required in any horsemanship class. In other words, you must not only demonstrate correct riding form on your own part but you must also be able to maneuver your horse easily while keeping this form. Before you even think of entering a national horse show, you must be able to canter a horse on the correct 'lead.' What is a lead? Well, when you get to the point of being able to canter, you'll notice that in this gait the horse always leads with one of his front feet at every stride. If he is on the right lead, his right front leg always strikes out ahead of the left. The opposite is true if the horse is cantering on the left lead; then his left foot will extend ahead of the others. When cantering in a ring, the leg toward the center of the ring should lead first. To put the horse on the correct lead, you turn his head slightly toward the rail (away from the center of the ring) and kick with your foot nearest the rail. The horse should break into the canter on the correct lead when you give those signals. He should *not* be run into a canter from the trot. Learn to change leads easily and quickly; then practice doing figure eights and performing serpentines. This will give you added drill in changing leads.

You should also be able to back your

Complex jumps give horses rigid test   *Formal top hats go with shadbelly coats*

The competition is stiff in jumping classes. It takes top-notch riding form to win at the Garden

Handsome, high-stepping hackney
ponies are judged on looks,
way of moving, performance, and
manners. Carts are called gigs

These are Lippizaners, famed white horses of Vienna.
Seen here at the Garden, they are considered among
most beautiful and highly trained horses in the world

Good form and competence with
mount may take you to big
shows early. Here a young
rider takes jump on her prized pony

*Coaches and four are another
attraction at the Garden in addition to
the various horsemanship classes*

*Royal Canadian Mounted Police
and their horses perform drill
that shows importance of teamwork*

Frank Chapot, U.S. champion, in Rome for Olympics

horse easily when mounted, remembering to move your legs back slightly while pulling steadily and evenly on the reins. Diagonals are another technicality you should be familiar with. When you are trotting your horse in a riding ring, the motion of your posting should correspond to the movement of the horse's front legs. Every time his leg next to the rail goes forward, you should be going *up*. When his leg nearest the center goes forward, you should be down.

All these are skills you must acquire before entering the more advanced

horsemanship classes, or classes where the horse's performance is at stake. Practice the exercises every day until you have mastered them. Then try performing them without stirrups, being certain to keep your legs in the proper position.

Once you really become familiar with these requirements and are at ease doing them with or without stirrups, the road to the big show rings is not a long or difficult one. Let's take a visit to Madison Square Garden now—just to see what it will be like when *you* ride there.

Opening night at the National is truly a splendid affair, rivaled in elegance only by the opening of the Metropolitan Opera. The show takes place during the latter part of November, usually within a week of the opening of the Met. Each year there is a sort of delightful, unofficial competition between the opera and the horse show to see which opening will be the more spectacular.

The ring is in the form of a huge oval, brilliantly colored in orange and black along the sides. At each end hang the flags of the countries competing in the international jumping classes—usually at least eight nations. Every year the Garden looks forward to sporting the colors of our three most regular visitors—the Irish, the Mexicans, and the Canadians—but other nations competing in recent years include Chile, Germany, France, England, Italy, and Argentina.

At one end of the ring are the 'in'

Irish Army team rider completes beautiful jump as his horse stretches to clear hurdle

and 'out' gates—the entrance and exit to the ring used by the horses and riders. Over the 'out' gate is located the sparkling brass band which sends tingles through the viewers when it plays the national anthem of each country represented by its equestrian team.

At every performance there is a special exhibition in addition to the regular competitive classes. Often the scarlet-coated Royal Canadian Mounties go through their formations, or a special 'dressage' act will provide this extra entertainment. A dressage horse is a superbly trained animal capable of doing the most astounding feats at the slightest signal from its rider—a signal which is invisible, to most onlookers. First-nighters get an added treat for, on opening night only, there is a special march of the U. S. Army band which goes through intricate formations while playing stirring marches.

Then the classes begin, and the gleaming lights shine from above on each rider and his mount. The sleek coats of the horses reflect the lights with mirror-like brilliance. The ani-

89

You're up on top of the world
when you win a tri-color
championship ribbon at this show

Gleaming trophy is formally presented
member of U.S. Equestrian Team
as winners of international
jumping competition at the Garden

mals sense the excitement of the moment and, with ears perked forward and nostrils flaring, they circle the ring with special beauty. The atmosphere is tense and every muscle in every horse is taut—ready for a signal from the rider, ready to exert the ultimate in his strength to dash over a five-foot jump, or ready to strain every inch of his body in order to pick up his feet as high as he can, or rack just a little bit faster.

Riders are deep in concentration and, of course, dressed in their very best. Saddle-seat folk wear formal tuxedo saddle suits—black jodhpurs with a black satin stripe down the side of each leg, black jackets with satin lapels, black boots and black top hats made of silk. The handsome figure they cut is enough to make any operagoer think twice about whether his own attire is up to par! Picture what a stunning sight these riders are, dressed in black and mounted on their different-colored horses sporting gay brow and nose bands!

But hunter-seat riders are not to be outdone by their saddle-seat friends. Long forgotten are the blue jeans and loafers: the girls will have on their best canary-yellow breeches, shining black boots with patent leather tops, and snow-white stocks held with a plain gold pin. To this each will add the formal vest and dashing fitted, black shad-belly formal hunt coat with a collar matching the colors of the hunt each girl rides with. The shad-belly coat looks something like a man's full-dress tail coat except that it fastens in front instead of hanging loose. Of course, the outfit is completed with a silk top hat.

Men wear essentially the same attire, with slight differences in the cut of the formal coat and details of the boots.

As these riders and their big, intelligent-looking hunters flow smoothly over one jump after another, you'll feel that you are in another world, another time. You'll think you must be with the royal courtiers of an ancient English king, out on the bronzed autumn fields with a pack of hounds heralding the call of the wild, free spirit of the hunter.

When the last rider circles the ring, the class will be over. The judges will confer and the winners will be announced. You will feel yourself slipping back to the present as grooms and workmen buzz about getting ready for the next class. Then the winning horses return to the ring, and the polished, shimmering trophy goes to the best horse and rider.

The presentation is made by a lady in evening dress escorted by a gentleman also in full evening attire. . . . You see yourself as that winning rider, and know that this is the crowning glory. It is something out of a make-believe world—and yet you know it is real. It happens now, in our time—and you can see its splendor every single year. In fact, it is a spectacle of beauty all your very own once you've caught Horse Fever.

PAT JOHNSON

A native of New Rochelle, Pat Johnson started riding at the age of three and showing horses at the annual Hutchinson Farms Horse Show at nine. While in school, Pat concentrated her spare time on hunting, which she vastly enjoyed, and rode with the Old Chatham Hunt. During summers in school and college—she went to the Emma Willard School, then to Vassar and New York University—she taught riding to countless campers, and also worked on a horse breeding farm training young horses. Meanwhile, her sister Peg devoted week-ends to showing and went on to win, on her horse Peg's Pride, the Reserve Open Jumping Championship of the United States and Canada.

After college, Pat worked for two years in the editorial department of Sports Illustrated, then joined Fawcett Publications where she is now Associate Editor of Gold Medal Books.

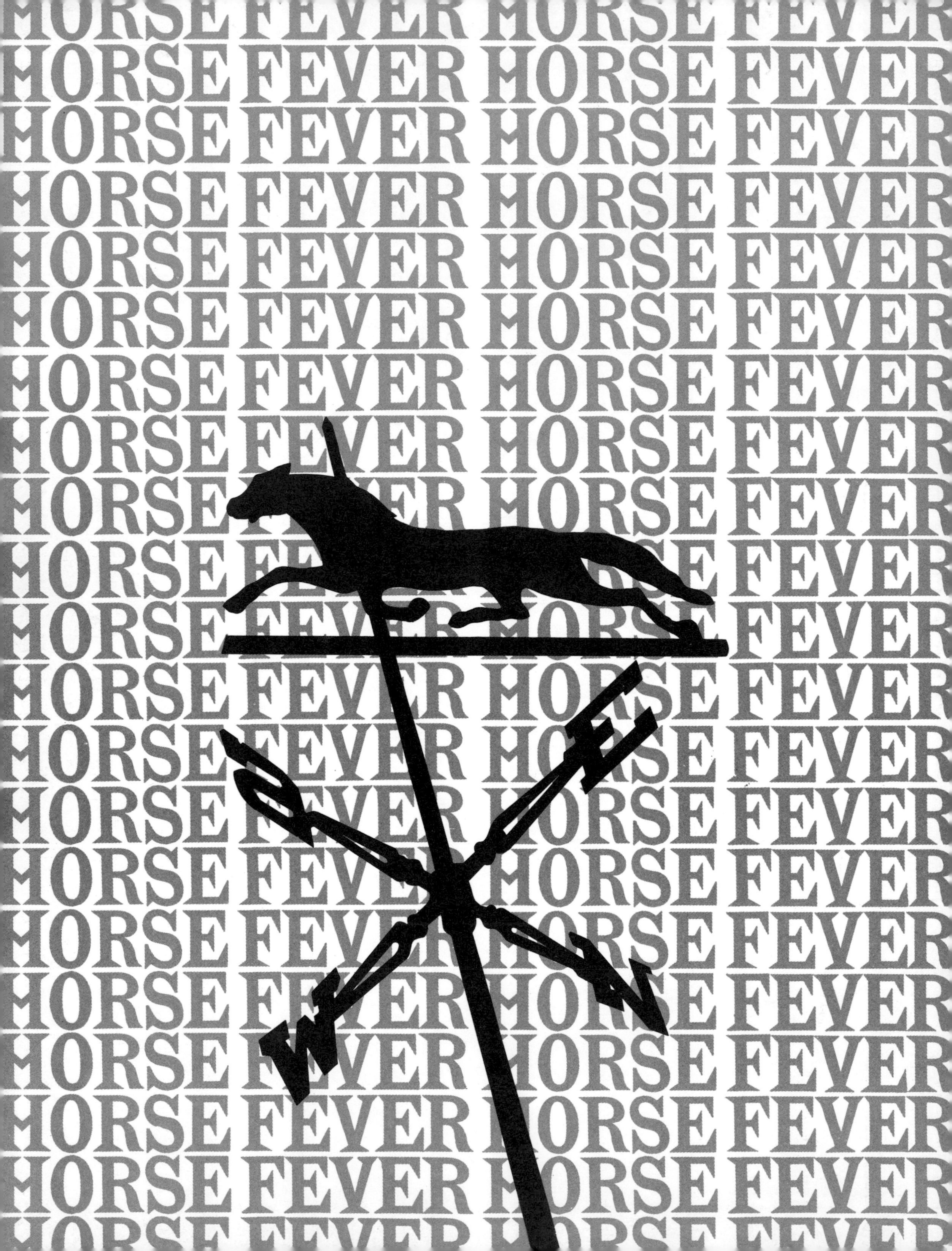
HORSE FEVER HORSE FEVER
E
S
W
N